THE SYMANTEC
HOME INTERNET
SECURITY

THE SYMANTEC GUIDE TO
HOME INTERNET
SECURITY

ANDREW CONRY-MURRAY
and
VINCENT WEAFER

✦✦Addison-Wesley

Upper Saddle River, NJ • Boston• Indianapolis • San Francisco
New York • Toronto • Montreal • London • Munich • Paris • Madrid
Capetown • Sydney • Tokyo • Singapore • Mexico City

Many of the designations used by manufacturers and sellers to distinguish their products are claimed as trademarks. Where those designations appear in this book, and the publisher was aware of a trademark claim, the designations have been printed with initial capital letters or in all capitals.

The authors and publisher have taken care in the preparation of this book but make no expressed or implied warranty of any kind and assume no responsibility for errors or omissions. No liability is assumed for incidental or consequential damages in connection with or arising from the use of the information or programs contained herein.

Publisher Symantec Press: Linda McCarthy
Editor in Chief: Karen Gettman
Acquisitions Editor: Jessica Goldstein
Cover Designer: Alan Clements
Managing Editor: Gina Kanouse
Project Editor: Christy Hackerd
Copy Editor: Gayle Johnson
Indexer: Julie Bess
Proofreader: Lisa Thibault
Compositor: Viewtistic, Inc.
Manufacturing Buyer: Dan Uhrig

The publisher offers excellent discounts on this book when ordered in quantity for bulk purchases or special sales, which may include electronic versions and/or custom covers and content particular to your business, training goals, marketing focus, and branding interests. For more information, please contact:

U.S. Corporate and Government Sales
800-382-3419
corpsales@pearsontechgroup.com

For sales outside the U.S., please contact:

International Sales
international@pearsoned.com

Visit us on the Web at www.awprofessional.com.

ISBN 0-321-35641-1

Text printed in the United States on recycled paper at R.R. Donnelley and Sons in Crawfordsville, Indiana.
First printing, September 2005

Library of Congress Cataloging-in-Publication Data
Conry-Murray, Andrew.
  The Symantec guide to home computer security / Andrew Conry-Murray and Vincent Weafer.
    p. cm.
  ISBN 0-321-35641-1
1. Computer security. 2. Internet–Security measures. I. Weafer, Vincent. II. Title.
QA76.9.A25C6677 2005
005.8–dc22

                                   2005016558

Table of Contents

Acknowledgments

First and foremost I want to thank my wife, Clare, who basically became a single parent in the midst of writing her doctoral dissertation and being pregnant to give me time to write this book. I couldn't have done it without her love, support, and encouragement. Thanks also to my son Aidan, who sacrificed many stories and much playtime for the sake of this book.

At Addison-Wesley I'd like to thank Jessica Goldstein for her enthusiasm for the project, and Frank Vella for keeping track of all the details. I'd also like to thank Jessica and Frank for shepherding a first-time author through the twin mazes of the publishing process and publishing contracts. As well, thanks to Audrey Doyle and Gayle Johnson for their sharp editorial eyes and insightful comments.

At Symantec I'd like to thank Linda McCarthy for this fantastic opportunity, and Vincent Weafer for his technological expertise, deep security knowledge, and hard work—particularly his ability to burrow into the tangled complexities surrounding spyware and emerge with a set of sensible definitions.

I'd also like to thank my colleagues past and present at *Network Magazine/IT Architect*. In particular, I'd like to thank Steve Steinke and Elizabeth Clark for giving me my start as an editor and writer and letting me cut my teeth on the security beat. I'd also like to thank Art Wittmann, Andy Dornan, Nancy Hung, David Greenfield, Doug Allen, Haig MacGregor, and John Angel. They all have helped me learn the ins and outs of innumerable networking and computer technologies and have shown me how to be a better writer, both through example and via excellent (although perhaps not always graciously received) critiques.

Finally, I'd like to thank my parents, my sister, and the extended Ouellette, Murray, Conry, and Smith clans for every conceivable form of love and support, including (but not limited to) intellectual stimulation, cash, housing, music, care packages, hospitality, and liturgical dance.

—Andrew Conry-Murray

I would like to thank Andrew for all his hard work and dedication on this book and for his neverending patience with the many updates and changes that came his way. I would also like to thank the team at Symantec for helping to review the book and making its messages clearer and more understandable. A special thanks to Jessica and Frank at Addison-Wesley and Linda McCarthy at Symantec for keeping us all on track. On a personal level, I wanted to thank my wife, Caitriona, and family David, Sinead, and Roghan for bearing with the many late nights spent working on security incidents that went into building up the experiences for this book.

—Vincent Weafer

About the Authors

Andrew Conry-Murray is the technology editor at *IT Architect,* an award-winning publication for information technology professionals. He has been writing about computer and network security since 2000.

Vincent Weafer has an extensive range of experience, gained from more than 20 years in the information technology industry, ranging from software development, systems engineering, to security research positions. For the past eight years, he has been the operational leader of the Symantec Global Security Response team, where his mission is to advance the research into new computer security threats and provide security content solutions such as anti-virus, anti-spam, intrusion and vulnerability response, real-time alerting, content solutions, research, and analysis.

Weafer has also been one of Symantec's main spokespeople on Internet security threats and trends, with national and international press and broadcast media, appearing on CBS, ABC, NBC, CNN, and BBC, among many others. In addition, he has presented at many international conferences on security threats and trends, presenting papers and contributing to technical panels run by the European Institute for Computer AntiVirus Research (EICAR), Virus Bulletin, Association of AntiVirus Asia Researchers (AVAR), and Australian Computer Emergency Response Team (AUSCERT), among many others.

Introduction

Thank you for picking up this book. If you're looking for quick and easy solutions to keeping your Windows-based computers safe from the dark side of the Internet, this is it. This book is especially for nontechnical users, so it includes a host of step-by-step instructions and helpful figures. If you know how to surf the Web and download software, you have all the skills you need to gain the benefits of a safe and secure Internet experience.

Today more and more of us conduct sensitive transactions via e-mail and the Internet, including online banking, stock trading, e-commerce purchasing, and personal accounts management. While the Internet makes such activities more convenient, it also exposes us to security risks. Traditional risks such as viruses, worms, and Trojan horses still plague the Internet. In addition, a new set of threats has emerged, including spyware, Internet fraud, and spam. These headline-grabbing threats, which are driven by profit-motivated criminals, are becoming increasingly sophisticated, have shorter life cycles, and use new attack vectors. Such threats pose daunting new challenges for everyone who uses the Internet.

Even seemingly safe information and entertainment sites can carry risks. For example, in a study conducted by Internet security company Symantec, researchers took a brand-new Windows PC, plugged it into the Internet without any security software, and browsed the Web. Testers spent one hour each interacting with different categories of Web sites, including e-commerce, gaming, and news sites. Surprisingly, children's Web sites dumped the most unwanted software onto the test PC—359 pieces of adware in just an hour's surfing!

The primary goal of this book is to help you understand that using the Internet carries a certain amount of risk—to your privacy, to the integrity of your personal data, and to your computer's usability and performance. We clearly explain those risks and show you, in simple but comprehensive detail, how to reduce your exposure.

Unlike other computer security books that focus on one or two problems such as viruses or spam, this book is intended to be a comprehensive resource for the broad range of risks that Internet users face. You'll find a wealth of information about how to keep your Windows computer free of spyware, worms, viruses, spam, and intruders; use e-mail and Web browsers safely; help protect your identity and privacy; protect a wireless connection from eavesdroppers and scammers; and shield your kids from pornography and online predators.

If you flip through the chapters or look at the table of contents, you'll see that this book includes loads of details—including figures and step-by-step instructions—about how to choose and use a wide variety of security software, how to take advantage of the security features built into Windows XP Service Pack 2, and how to protect yourself and your family from the criminals and con artists trolling for victims. Many of the software tools and programs recommended in this book are free.

This book is designed to help you solve specific problems so that you don't have to read it from start to finish. You can start with any chapter about any one of the risks you're most concerned about and get all the information you need. Of course, many Internet risks are intertwined, so this book provides references to other relevant chapters.

The Internet is often compared to a superhighway, but it's more like a city—one where we are spending more and more of our lives. It's also a city of almost infinite size and serious dangers. This book is designed to be a trusted guide to this city so that you and your family can enjoy a safe and secure Internet experience.

Chapter 1

Understanding Internet Risk

Try to imagine life without the Internet. In just a few short years this technology has become indispensable; we rely on it for communication, entertainment, information, and commerce. The Internet and the World Wide Web make our lives more enjoyable and productive.

Unfortunately, the Internet has also become indispensable to thieves, vandals, and con artists. The Internet and the Web are under attack from a growing number of criminals who use the power of this global network to destroy your files, invade your privacy, hijack or crash your computer, and even steal your money and ruin your credit.

But while the risks are real, they aren't insurmountable. Tools and techniques are available to thwart these dangers, so you don't have to turn your back on all the Internet has to offer. And with this book as your guide, you also don't have to become a security expert; if you've ever used a Web browser or installed software, you have all the skills you need to protect yourself and your family.

One way to think of the problem is to compare your computer to a car. Every time you drive, you assume certain risks: Your car may break down, you might get in an accident, or you might even be killed. You accept these risks because of the great benefits your car provides, and because steps have been taken to mitigate those risks: Your car has brakes, seat belts, and airbags. You've had driving lessons. And you've taken out car insurance.

Every time you use the Internet, you also accept certain risks: identity theft, viruses, spam, spyware, and so on. Even seemingly harmless sites such as well-known e-commerce destinations or online entertainment sites may infest your computer with software that generates advertising (and degrades your PC's performance) or tracks your Internet usage. However, many people are using the Internet without taking any steps to mitigate those risks: no firewall, no anti-virus software, and no idea that fraudsters and hijackers are actively trolling the Internet for new victims. This is akin to driving without brakes or a seat belt. The goal of this book is to help you understand what risks the Internet poses and to give you the information you need to address those risks.

This chapter looks at the most pressing Internet risks and explains why home PCs are attractive targets for Internet criminals. However, keep in mind that in addition to being exposed to criminal activity, using the Internet presents risks to the family such as access to unwanted content like pornography or to activities such as online gambling or the illegal sharing of copyrighted music and movies. Unsecured wireless connections at home or at public wireless "hotspots" can also expose your private information to anyone with a wireless-enabled laptop. We'll address these topics in later chapters.

1.1 Fraudsters and Hijackers

Attacks against home users generally fall into two basic classes: fraud and hijacking. Computer fraud attempts to separate you from your money by offering shady products via e-mail or pop-up ads or by tricking you into revealing personal information or financial account data such as passwords. Identity theft, phishing, and spam are prime examples of computer fraud.

Hijackers attempt to take control of your computer for nefarious purposes, such as tracking your online activity, serving up unwanted advertising, degrading the performance of your computer or Internet connection, or recruiting your computer to send spam or launch attacks against other targets on the Internet. Criminals rely heavily on malware (software programs that are used for malicious purposes) to hijack computers. Malware includes viruses, worms, Trojan horses, spyware, and adware. In some cases, criminals combine fraud and hijacking to achieve their goals. This section reviews the most common Internet threats.

Identity Theft

One of today's most prevalent and fastest-growing Internet threats is identity theft—the loss of information such as bank and credit account numbers, passwords, and Social Security numbers. This information can be used to commit fraud either online or offline.

According to the Federal Trade Commission, nearly 10 million Americans were victims of identity theft in 2003. In extreme cases, financial losses range into the tens of thousands of dollars. Victims can have their credit ratings ruined, and it can take months of effort to recover.

Phishing attacks are a form of identity theft that relies on e-mail and the Web. Here's how it works. You receive an e-mail claiming to be from a major bank, credit card company, or e-commerce site. The e-mail says there is a problem with your account and asks you to send your username, account number, and password to confirm your account status. However, this e-mail is bogus. You actually are mailing this sensitive information to a scam artist, most likely someone overseas.

An updated version of this scam includes a Web link in the e-mail. If you click the link you see a log-in page that looks identical to the log-in page of your bank, credit card company, or e-commerce Web site, including the business's logo. After you type in your information you see an error message or perhaps are asked to enter your information twice. In the meantime, the log-in information is sent to a server under the scam artists' control. They use this information to make purchases or withdraw money in your name. They also might sell your personal information to other criminals.

Spam

According to some estimates, unsolicited e-mail (better known as spam) now accounts for 80 percent of all e-mail traffic on the Internet. While spam isn't as significant a threat as malware or identity theft in terms of harm, it's certainly one of the Internet's biggest nuisances. You have to waste your time deleting unwanted mail, and the messages are often filled with offensive language or images. Identity thieves also use spam techniques to send fraudulent e-mail.

Viruses and Worms

A virus is self-replicating code that lives inside a host body, such as a Word document. A worm is a self-replicating program that transmits itself from computer to computer. Worms and viruses often contain malicious payloads that can hijack your computer, destroy files, or steal personal information. Research indicates that 500 new viruses and worms are released onto the Internet every week. Every year the number of viruses and worms on the Internet grows by 400 percent. And Internet criminals are getting better at creating fast-spreading worms. For instance, in 2004 the Blaster worm infected 100,000 computers in just five hours. An even faster worm, the SQL Slammer, propagated so quickly that the number of computers it infected doubled in size every 8.5 seconds during its first minute of life.

Spyware, Adware, and Trojan Horses

Spyware is another growing category of malware. The term "spyware" is often used as a general descriptor for a set of programs that have various capabilities, such as changing the phone number your modem dials when you go online, collecting your keystrokes, or redirecting your browser to unwanted sites.

Adware is a separate but closely related class of programs. Adware collects information about you and your Web surfing habits to serve up targeted advertising. Adware programs can fill your computer screen with pop-up ads, redirect you to strange search sites, and seriously degrade your computer's performance.

Unlike viruses and worms, spyware and adware don't self-replicate. These programs get deposited on your PC without your knowledge. This can happen when you visit a Web site that surreptitiously downloads the program to your computer. Spyware and adware may also come bundled with free utilities such as screen savers, weather trackers, and browser toolbars. Software that lets you share music and video files is a persistent source of adware. According to an Earthlink survey, the average home PC has up to 25 spyware and adware programs residing on it.

Then there are Trojan horses. These software programs are named after the legendary Trojan horse inside which Greek soldiers hid to smuggle themselves into the heavily fortified city of Troy. When the horse was safely behind Troy's walls, the Greek soldiers waited until nightfall and then snuck out, murdered Troy's soldiers in their beds, and captured the city.

Today's Trojan horses won't stab you while you sleep, but they can give a remote attacker full and complete control over your machine. The attacker can read, change, and delete your files; launch programs; install or remove software; and generally make your computing life miserable.

1.2 Why Me?

It's a mistake to think you're safe from Internet crime, even if the only things on your computer are vacation photos, some MP3 downloads, a few work documents, and your secret diary. While it's true that the contents of any individual hard drive aren't of interest to bad guys, the appeal to Internet criminals is one of scale: They aren't just attacking you; they're attacking thousands or hundreds of thousands of other machines simultaneously.

Scale is important for two reasons. First, compromised machines themselves become resources for attacking still more computers. Second, the more potential victims a fraudster can reach, the more chances that someone will fall for the scam. Let's look at these ideas separately.

Your Computer Is a Resource for Attacking Other Computers

Your PC and its Internet connection are valuable targets because, when combined with hundreds or thousands of others, they can become a weapon that the attacker can use against someone else, often a business or government target. Automated software tools scan wide swaths of the Internet, looking for vulnerable machines. Automated intrusion tools then use the same exploit over and over, installing malicious programs that give the attacker remote control over an army of machines. These hijacked computers are often called "zombies" or "bots."

Internet criminals have many uses for zombies. First, attackers use large numbers of zombies to launch denial-of-service (DoS) attacks. DoS attacks work by sending an overwhelming amount of network traffic to a target, such as a corporate or government Web site. A large-enough DoS attack can knock the target site offline.

Internet criminals also use DoS attacks as a form of Internet extortion: Web site owners are threatened with an attack and are told to pay up or face having their site shut down. Such scams are often effective if the target site prefers not to enlist the help of law enforcement. Porn sites, gambling sites, and other vice-related locales are prime targets for this kind of attack.

Other software can turn your PC into a spamming machine. Spamming has become a hit-and-run operation. Spammers continually search for new machines from which to send their junk mail because Internet service providers (ISPs) and anti-spam organizations are quick to identify and block any computers that send junk mail. One spammer trick is to break into home computers and use them to send thousands or millions of messages, and then move on. The problem for you is that your own e-mail won't be delivered because your computer has been labeled as a source of spam.

Some groups, including organized crime, maintain large farms of compromised computers. They rent these hijacked machines to the highest bidder to use them for launching DoS attacks or sending spam. PCs with high-speed, always-on Internet connections are particularly valuable to criminals.

Last but not least is good old status. A fast-spreading virus or worm earns notoriety for its creator or creators. The more machines that are compromised, the better the bragging rights.

Your Computer Is a Communication Vehicle for Frauds and Scams

In the real world, a con artist usually can approach only one potential victim at a time. On the Internet, the number of potential victims is almost limitless. The Internet also makes it easy for criminals to hide their identities while running scams that can reach around the world.

E-mail makes the job even simpler, because even well-protected computers accept electronic messages. E-mail scams, phishing, and spam have a low rate of return (that is, only 1 or 2 percent of the total recipients respond), but if you can send hundreds of thousands of messages (or millions of messages in the case of spam), your results can still generate profits.

A popular e-mail scam has fraudsters posing as relatives of former African oil ministers. These "relatives" want your help in moving millions of dollars out of the country, with a tidy percentage of those millions offered in payment for your assistance. All you have to do is give them your bank account number, and maybe send a few thousand dollars up front to help them process "paperwork."

On a recent trip to West Africa, I actually saw five men in a cybercafe sending out hundreds of such e-mails, all of them claiming to be from the wife of a deposed government bigwig. I tried to interview one of them because it would've made a great story, but he shut down his computer and said he was only writing to friends. Right. Be aware that oil-producing companies in Africa aren't the only lure: Iraq and former states of the Soviet Union are also used as bait, as are countries that have recently suffered natural disasters.

In another variation on this scheme, con artists pretend to be a woman in Russia. They start conversations with men who post profiles on Internet dating services. They provide photos (inevitably the woman is attractive) and engage in detailed correspondence. Soon the "woman" confesses her love and expresses a desire to meet. She is sweetly embarrassed to have to ask for money to help defray the cost of the visa, or the airline ticket, or whatever. In the end, gullible victims lose hundreds, even thousands, of dollars.

Subsequent chapters examine the best ways to protect against these persistent Internet threats.

Chapter 2

Preventing Identity Theft

Your ability to prove your identity—that is, to prove you are who you say you are—is essential to the way in which the world conducts commerce. You use proof of identity to authenticate yourself to the organization with which you are doing business and to authorize services or transactions. Picture IDs, whether on a driver's license or a credit card, are the most common way to verify identities in the real world.

On the Internet, your identity consists of many elements, such as usernames, passwords, personal identification numbers (PINs), your Social Security number, various account numbers, and your mother's maiden name. These digital identities operate on the assumption that you're the only person who knows this information. This is a poor assumption, and it makes fraud trivial to perpetrate. When you're conducting business online, no one can ask you for a photo ID.

In the early days of the Internet, the worst outcome of identity theft was that your username and password for your Internet service provider (ISP) could be stolen, which meant that someone else could surf the Internet on your dime.

Today we use the Internet to conduct all kinds of financial transactions, which raises the stakes for identity theft. Criminals can use your digital identity to open credit card accounts, change your address (so that you don't start seeing strange credit card bills), take out bank loans, get mortgages, and conduct financial transactions, all in your name. They also can sell stolen identities to other criminals on a well-established Internet black market. Potential consequences run the gamut from a damaged credit rating to money being stolen from your bank account.

Credit card fraud is the most common form of identity theft. Thieves steal personal information that they use to open accounts in someone else's name, run up a month or two of charges, and simply abandon the card once the credit company pulls the plug. According to a story in the *New York Times*,[1] one identity theft ring stole upward of 30,000 identities and made tens of millions of dollars during a two-year period by reselling merchandise bought with fraudulent credit cards. This criminal ring was so successful because they bribed an employee of a company that had access to consumers' digital identities. This malicious insider used his access to harvest digital identities, which he sold to a gang who opened fraudulent accounts.

Profits can be made from even small numbers of stolen identities. In 2004, a Virginia man pled guilty to stealing the names and personal information of 10 people. He used that information to open credit accounts and purchase more than $85,000 worth of merchandise, which he then resold on eBay.

While the bad guys make purchases or abscond with the loan money, you are stuck with the bills. Even if you aren't held responsible for them, you have to undergo the arduous procedure of restoring your credit history.

This chapter looks at how criminals can steal your identity, lists steps you can take to prevent identity theft, and gives you tips on how to recover if your identity gets stolen and misused.

2.1 How Your Identity Gets Stolen

There are two ways for your digital identity to be stolen. One way is for information about you to be stolen from the databases of the banks, ISPs, retailers, data clearinghouses, and other entities that store such information. Sometimes this information is stolen by highly skilled computer criminals. For instance, in June 2005, it was reported that computer criminals stole account information on more than 200,000 credit cards from CardSystem Solutions, a credit card payment processor. Information from as many as 40 million cards may also have been exposed by the attack. More often, thefts are facilitated by an employee or business partner who has access to the data, as in the case announced in the spring of 2005 in which employees at four banks, including Bank of America and

---

1. *Gone in 60 Seconds: Identity Theft is Epidemic. Can It Be Stopped?"* by Timothy L. O'Brien, New York Times, October 24, 2004.

Wachovia, sold more than 670,000 customer account records to a thief. Finally, identity information can be acquired through good old fashioned scams. In one recent case, thieves simply posed as legitimate businesses to get access to identity data from ChoicePoint, a data clearinghouse. Rather than executing a complex "hack," the thieves simply obtained California business licenses and then bought customer information through ChoicePoint's regular channels. (For more information about how the ChoicePoint breach came to light, see the sidebar near the end of this chapter, "Compelling Companies to Report Privacy Breaches.") As a computer user, there's very little you can do to protect yourself against this kind of identity theft other than to monitor your bank and credit card statements for odd transactions, check your credit history regularly, and be choosy about the companies with which you do business. In some cases you can check whether information about you is being stored by data clearinghouse companies. See Chapter 10, "Privacy and the Internet," for more information.

The second way to steal your identity is for the attacker to steal the information directly from you, or to trick you into giving him the information. In many cases this is much easier for the attacker than trying to break into a well-defended network (although hacking into corporate databases can be disturbingly easy for knowledgeable and persistent intruders, but that's a subject for another book).

In most cases you can do something about this second method of identity theft. But before we cover that, here's some information about the different ways in which identity theft is perpetrated.

Social Engineering

Social engineering is a fancy way to describe tricking people. Social engineering relies on our innate trust of other people (OK, gullibility), especially in the presence of particular social cues, such as a uniform and badge, or a business suit.

Criminals and professional security experts (sometimes called penetration testers) use social engineering when attempting to breach a secure location. For instance, penetration testers wear a suit and tie to an office and just wander around to see what they can find. Rarely does anyone challenge them. For instance, have you ever asked to see a stranger's employee badge if he follows you through a door that requires the use of a keycard? If you did challenge him and he said he left his badge at his desk, what would you do then? Most likely you'd nod and smile and let him through.

Perhaps the most infamous social engineer is Kevin Mitnick, a convicted criminal whose greatest exploits were often facilitated not by his programming skills or a bag of computer tricks, but by a telephone. One of his favorite targets was the phone company. He would call the phone company pretending to be an engineer and get the person on the other end of the line to provide him with all sorts of useful information, such as passwords that would give him access to sensitive computer systems. You can read more about Mitnick's exploits and how he was caught in *Takedown: The Pursuit and Capture of Kevin Mitnick, America's Most Wanted Computer Outlaw—By the Man Who Did It*, by Tsutomu Shimomura and John Markoff.

Many identity theft scams rely on some degree of social engineering. The most common vehicles are fraudulent e-mails that purport to come from a legitimate organization, or free Internet goodies such as file-sharing software, games, or utilities that also contain malicious programs that can be used to steal confidential information.

Spoofing

On the Internet, to spoof means to create a bogus or fake version of something such as a Web site or e-mail address. For instance, many identity thieves set up fraudulent Web sites that look identical to the real thing and trick users into going to these sites. Once at the site, users log in with their usernames and passwords, which the criminals gather and use to get access to the real Web site. This is known as Web site spoofing. Spammers also spoof return e-mail addresses—that is, they include a return e-mail address in their spam messages that doesn't actually exist.

Phishing Attacks

Phishing attacks are the most prominent, and most damaging, of today's Internet frauds. Many phishing attacks start with an e-mail. For example, a criminal syndicate sends thousands of spam messages that purport to be from a bank, credit card company, ISP, or e-commerce company (eBay and PayPal are two popular targets). Some phishing e-mail is an obvious scam, but other messages are works of art, complete with the company logo and written in the language of corporate marketing.

Phishing messages generally sound alike. They say there's a problem with your account that you must take care of immediately, and they include a link to what looks like the Web site's sign-in page. In fact, the site is a fake. This fake site is an exact duplicate of the real site, but it's hosted on servers that belong to the criminals. In other cases, the link may be legitimate, but the criminals have manipulated the Internet addressing system to redirect you to their fraudulent site (this is sometimes called "pharming").

If you click the link, you find a log-on page that looks identical to the regular site, complete with fields to enter your username, account number, and password. Many spoofed sites get greedy and ask for other information, like your Social Security number. Wanting to address any problems with your account, you—the victim—dutifully type in the information. Depending on how clever the identity thieves are, they may actually transfer you to the real site. Less-clever thieves present you with an error message. In the meantime, your information has been transmitted to a server under the control of the criminals.

As if this weren't bad enough, phishers are getting more clever. Many are including malicious software programs in the e-mail they send. These programs can do different things. Some programs are keystroke loggers (which are discussed next). Other programs instruct your computer to go to a spoofed site even if you type the Web address of a legitimate site into the browser. One program has been discovered that has a list of banking sites. If you go to one of the sites on its list, after you log in, the program opens an invisible browser behind the one you see on your screen. The program then checks your balance and transfers money to an account under the criminal's control.

Even more worrisome is a growing class of attacks in which a criminal has corrupted the actual sign-in page of a legitimate Web site. That is, you could type **www.yourbank.com** into your browser and be directed to the legitimate site. But when you type in your information, malicious code previously inserted into the Web site by criminals captures that information and sends it to computers under their control. This is a frightening development, because even if you do everything right, flaws in how legitimate sites are created leave them open to this attack, and there is nothing you can do about it.

Keystroke Loggers

Keystroke loggers are programs that keep track of every key you press on your keyboard. This information is sent to a remote attacker, who scans the information for useful bits of data such as passwords and account numbers. Some keystroke loggers come with a list of Web sites, such as banks and e-commerce sites, and they start recording keystrokes only when you type those URLs into a browser. Keystroke loggers are discussed a bit more in Chapter 5, "Getting Rid of Unwanted Guests, Part 2: Spyware, Adware, and Trojan Horses." They are used primarily to perpetrate identity theft.

Mail Theft and Dumpster Diving

Identity thieves can steal incoming and outgoing mail right out of your mailbox. Just think of all the useful information contained inside a credit card payment envelope: your name, address, phone number, credit card number, and checking account number. If you can, get a lockable box for incoming mail, and drop your outgoing letters into a city mailbox.

A less savory but still effective tactic is called dumpster diving. People throw away all kinds of interesting and potentially useful information, such as bank and credit account statements. Attackers can pick up this information simply by rifling through your trash or recyclables. It's about as low-tech as you can get, but it works. The best way to prevent dumpster diving is to shred any sensitive documents before disposing of them.

Speaking of throwing things away, you should take the time to wipe the hard drive of any computer you get rid of. Simply deleting files or formatting the hard disk isn't sufficient; numerous software programs exist that can recover "deleted" information. You need special software that turns your hard drive into a jumble of unintelligible data. Such tools include Web Eraser, WipeDrive, and O&O SafeErase. A company called WindsorTech can erase a hard drive over the Internet. See www.eraseyourharddrive.com.

2.2 Preventing Identity Theft

There are several ways to prevent online identity theft. Some involve the use of technology, but most rely on common sense. We'll start with commonsense prevention because it's effective and free. Then we'll move on to the technology options.

Think Before You Click

As mentioned, many identity theft scams rely on social engineering and fraudulent e-mail. Your best defense against these kinds of attacks is a healthy skepticism for any message that claims to come from an e-commerce site or financial institution. The following points can help you thwart e-mail-based phishing attacks:

- Legitimate organizations do not send e-mail that asks you for account information.

- Corporations take great care to avoid spelling and grammar mistakes in their communications with customers. Be wary of messages with spelling or grammar mistakes and odd phrasings.

- Do not click any links included with the message. Look carefully at these links. They may have odd extensions.

- If you are concerned that there really may be a problem with your account, your best option is to pick up the phone and call customer service. If that's not possible, close the e-mail and type the URL into your Web browser yourself. Don't cut and paste the URL from the e-mail.

- Use software or another tool, as described later in this chapter, to see if the site is spoofed.

- If you get e-mail claiming to be from a bank or e-commerce site that you don't do business with, delete the e-mail without opening it. Many phishing e-mails contain viruses or other malware that can infect your computer if you open the e-mail.

- Use anti-virus software, keep it updated, and make sure it's configured to scan your e-mail automatically.

- Check your bank and credit card statements regularly. You also may want to examine your credit report for unusual activity. You can purchase a credit report from the three major credit reporting agencies—Experian, Equifax, and TransUnion—but these organizations are also required by law to provide you with a free credit report once a year. To get a free copy, go to www.annualcreditreport.com or go to the individual sites of the reporting agencies. Your report can be provided online or sent via U.S. mail. You can order your free report over the phone by calling 877-322-8228.

Tools That Help Prevent Identity Theft

Besides common sense, numerous tools can help prevent identity theft. At the top of the list are anti-virus and anti-spyware programs. Because many phishing e-mails include viruses or malicious code, you need to keep your AV software updated. You should also invest in anti-spyware software (or make sure your anti-virus software includes spyware detection) and scan your machine regularly. Anti-spyware software can detect the kinds of programs, like keystroke loggers, that identity thieves use to get your personal data. Spyware and anti-spyware solutions are covered in greater detail in Chapter 5.

You also should take steps to make your Web browser more secure from so-called "drive-by downloads," in which malware is installed on your computer without your knowledge by malicious or compromised Web sites. Web browser security is covered in Chapter 7, "Securing Windows."

Other tools deal specifically with phishing and identity theft. The following sections discuss a few you might want to check out. Some are free, and others you have to pay for.

SSL

Secure Socket Layer (SSL) is the protocol that enables encrypted transmission of information sent via HTTP. (HTTP stands for Hypertext Transfer Protocol, the communications mechanism for the Web.) SSL also enables the use of digital certificates so that your Web browser can check a Web site's authenticity. A digital certificate is a form of electronic authentication that says a third party has verified that the holder of the certificate is who it claims to be. When you surf to your banking site and sign in to conduct a transaction, your Web browser looks at the site's digital certificate to ensure that www.onlinebank.com is in fact www.onlinebank.com. All Web browsers come preloaded with the ability to use SSL—there's nothing you need to do to turn it on.

There are two ways to tell if SSL is in use. The address in the browser bar says https:// rather than http://. (HTTPS is the secure version of Hypertext Transfer Protocol.) You also see a lock icon in the bottom-right corner of your Web browser.

However, be aware that the presence of the lock icon or https in the browser bar does not guarantee that the site isn't fraudulent. Identity thieves can register a site and use SSL just as easily as a legitimate business. While you should conduct transactions online only with Web sites that use SSL, not every site using SSL is a legitimate business.

Also, just because a legitimate business uses SSL to protect your data in transit, there's no guarantee that it will safely store your information. As noted, thieves regularly pillage corporate databases to steal information. This shouldn't necessarily turn you off to e-commerce, because the account numbers of the credit cards you use at real-world stores are also sitting in hackable databases. The problem isn't secure transmission—the problem is the difficulty of secure storage and procedural safeguards.

Security Tokens

As mentioned earlier, one problem with e-commerce is that its authentication system relies on information such as usernames and passwords that can be easily guessed or acquired by scammers. This problem can be addressed by two-factor authentication, which combines something you know (a username or password) with something you have. One example of two-factor authentication is an ATM card. The first factor is your PIN (something you know). The second factor is the bank card itself (something you have). Your PIN is useless to a criminal without your card, just as your card is useless without the PIN.

Two-factor authentication is especially useful for thwarting online identity theft because even if a thief can steal your username and password, he or she can't use your account without possessing the other factor.

In high-security corporate or government settings, two-factor authentication is accomplished with one of three items: a smart card, a biometric, or a token. A smart card is a credit-card-sized piece of plastic. It contains a computer chip that stores a digital certificate that uniquely identifies the holder of the card, and it is accessed with a PIN. A biometric is a digitized version of a physical characteristic such as a fingerprint or a scan of an eye's retina or iris. A token is a small device that generates a random number at regular intervals; users type in the number along with their log-on name and password.

When it comes to consumer e-commerce, tokens are likely to be the first widely deployed two-factor authentication mechanism. That's because smart cards and biometrics require special readers that have to be installed on a user's PC. Over time, more PCs will be sold with these devices built in, but for now tokens are easier to deploy to consumers because they require no additional hardware on the PC.

The best-known token is called SecurID, made by a security company called RSA. The SecurID token looks like a tiny pocket calculator with a small screen and no buttons. The token generates a new six-digit number at prescribed intervals (such as every 60 seconds). It generates each six-digit code through the use of a mathematical algorithm that combines a unique number called a seed value with a clock time. Every individual token has its own seed value, so no two tokens ever produce the same number.

When a user wants to log into a site that uses two-factor authentication, he or she is prompted to enter the six-digit number along with his or her username and password. A server owned by the organization has been programmed to know the seed value and clock time for each token, so it can tell if the six-digit code is valid.

The server also knows which user is associated with each token, so it can match the user ID to the six-digit code generated by the token. Finally, the server accepts only six-digit numbers that have been generated within a specific time frame (for example, within the last 5 minutes).

So how do tokens help prevent identity theft? Let's say a thief sends an e-mail asking for the user's log-in information. Even if the user sends the information, it's useless without the token code. And even if the user sends an attacker his or her password and the current number on the token's screen, that number likely will be useless by the time the attacker tries to use it.

Subscribers to America Online's premium broadband service have the option to purchase PassCode, which is a SecurID token being resold by AOL. Users enter the code number along with their username and password every time they sign on to their AOL account. At the time this book was published, AOL was charging $9.95 for the token plus a monthly fee of $1.95. The online brokerage firm E*Trade also offers a token to its customers. Banks and other service providers may make similar offers in the future.

However, while security tokens provide greater security than simple passwords, they do have drawbacks. The first issue is scale. Just imagine if every bank, ISP, and e-commerce company you do business with issued you a token. Every time you wanted to do a transaction online, you'd have to root around in a drawer full of tokens to find the right one. Tokens also eventually use up their battery life, and they can be lost, stolen, or broken.

A more serious problem is the increasing sophistication of attackers. Two-factor authentication won't help if there's a malicious program on your computer that simply waits until you log in. Or scammers could set up a fraudulent Web site that passes along your information (including the code from the token) to the real site and logs in on your behalf. Either way, the effect is the same: The attacker would have access to your account during a legitimate session and could conduct transactions. As security experts have discovered in the corporate world, the best strategy is defense in depth, such as using a token in addition to maintaining your computer's safety with security software.

SpoofStick

SpoofStick is a small program called a browser extension that can help you spot fake Web sites. It creates a new toolbar in your browser that shows you which Web site you are currently surfing. For instance, if you go to www.ebay.com, the SpoofStick toolbar says "You're on ebay.com." If you go to a Web site that only pretends to be eBay, SpoofStick reports only the IP address (for example, it says "You're on 192.1.2.3."). If SpoofStick shows you an IP address rather than the actual domain name, chances are high that the site you are surfing is not associated with the organization it claims to be associated with.

The same day I downloaded SpoofStick, I received an e-mail telling me that my eBay account needed to be updated. I knew the e-mail was a scam, because I don't have an eBay account, but I clicked the link provided in the e-mail to see if SpoofStick would spot the fake Web site. It did. Although both the fake e-mail and the spoofed Web page were masterful forgeries, SpoofStick wasn't fooled. The browser toolbar said "You're on..." and listed an IP address. After I deleted the fake message, I went surfing on the real eBay Web site, and on every page that I surfed, SpoofStick dutifully reported "You're on eBay.com."

SpoofStick was created by Phil Libin, president of CoreStreet, a computer security company. You can download it for both Internet Explorer and Mozilla Firefox at www.corestreet.com/spoofstick. Libin also runs a humorous blog (www.vastlyimportant.com) that's worth checking out.

2.3 Recovering from Identity Theft

Despite your best precautions, it's still possible to fall victim to identity thieves. (Remember, even if you never give out your account information, it still can be stolen from corporate or government data repositories, or even from your wallet or purse.) According to the Federal Trade Commission, nearly 10 million people were victims of identity theft in 2003.

Recovering from identity theft requires patience and persistence. Identity theft recovery experts recommend that you document all your interactions with the various businesses and agencies you work with, keep copies of all records, and follow up telephone calls with a letter to the company with which you are trying to resolve an identity theft case. Other tips are as follows:

- Report the theft to the bank, creditor, or service provider holding the fraudulent account. If someone opened a new account in your name, ask for the account to be closed. Ask to speak with a fraud investigator rather than a customer service representative. If someone has misused an existing account, report those unauthorized charges.
- Contact the major credit bureaus (Experian, Equifax, and TransUnion) to issue a fraud alert. The first time you issue a fraud alert to one of the

bureaus, it passes the alert to the other two. The fraud alert prevents new accounts from being opened in your name. See the next section for contact information.

- File a report with your local police department. Banks and credit card companies may require a police report before they proceed with remediation of identity theft, so ask for a copy of the report.

- Fill out an ID Theft Affidavit from the Federal Trade Commission (FTC). It can help you identify and collect all the information that likely will be requested by an organization investigating the fraud. To find a copy, go to www.consumer.gov/idtheft/ and click the ID Theft Affidavit link.

- Report the crime to the FTC, which maintains a database of identity theft reports. While the FTC will not assist you in recovering damages from your complaint, it does share complaint reports with law enforcement agencies, consumer credit agencies, and the organizations against which identity fraud is perpetrated. By reporting the theft, you help these organizations learn more about identity theft and how it can be resolved and prevented.

2.4 Checklist

Use this checklist as a quick-reference guide to the material covered in this chapter.

Do

- Request a free copy of your credit report annually. You can go to www.annualcreditreport.com or call 877-322-8228.

- Check your bank and credit card statements regularly for signs of unusual or suspicious activity.

- Be suspicious of any unsolicited contact (whether by phone or e-mail) that asks for sensitive information.

- Use anti-virus and anti-spyware software to prevent identity-stealing malware from invading your computer.

- Shred sensitive documents, including bank and credit card statements and credit card offers, before disposing of or recycling them.

- Place a fraud alert to the three major credit reporting agencies if you suspect or can confirm that your identity has been stolen:

Equifax, www.equifax.com, 888-766-0008

Experian, www.experian.com, 888-397-3742

TransUnion, www.transunion.com, 800-680-7289

- Fill out a police report and an ID Theft Affidavit if your identity has been stolen. You can find the ID Theft Affidavit at www.consumer.gov/idtheft/.

Don't

- Respond to e-mail that asks for personal identification information or account numbers.
- Click links embedded in e-mail that claims to come from your bank or e-commerce company.
- Open e-mail that claims to come from banks or e-commerce sites where you don't have accounts.
- Give out your Social Security number as an identifier if you don't have to.

2.5 Helpful Resources

This section presents additional resources to help you learn more.

Visa offers tips on protecting your digital identity and protecting yourself from other fraud, such as telephone fraud. Go to www.international.visa.com/ps/products/protect/main.jsp.

You can report phishing attempts to the FTC at spam@uce.gov. You can also file a complaint if you think you've been a victim of identity theft. Go to www.ftc.gov and clicking the File a Complaint link on the blue bar near the top of the page. To find out more about the other steps to take if you are a victim of identity theft, go to www.consumer.gov/idtheft, also run by the FTC. It contains extensive information about reporting the theft to credit agencies and law enforcement. You can also call the FTC's identity theft hotline at 877-IDTHEFT (877-438-4338) for information and advice.

If you are a victim of identity theft, you can file a complaint with the Internet Crime Complaint Center (IC3, www.ic3.gov). The IC3 is a joint venture between the FBI and the National White Collar Crime Center. Note that submitting a complaint does not mean that the FBI will take your case. Most likely the information will be used for research, but the complaint might be referred to a local law enforcement agency for further action. You can find a link to the complaint form at www.ic3.gov.

The Identity Theft Resource Center is a nonprofit group with information to help consumers prevent and recover from identity theft: www.idtheftcenter.org. Like the FTC, this center has helpful information on how to recover from identity theft. Click the Victim's Resources tab on the left side of the page.

The Anti-Phishing Working Group (APWG) is an association of businesses, service providers, computer security vendors, and law enforcement agencies. The APWG tracks phishing scams, keeps an archive of phishing e-mails, develops best-practices guidelines for businesses and consumers in preventing and responding to identity theft, and provides educational materials. If you're suspicious about an e-mail, check out the phishing archive. Go to www. anti-phishing.org and click the Phishing Archive link on the left side of the home page. You can also forward phishing e-mails to the group at reportphishing@antiphishing.org.

Compelling Companies to Report Privacy Breaches

On July 1, 2003, a new law known as California Senate Bill 1386 (SB 1386) went into effect. It compels companies with California customers to notify those customers about known or suspected disclosure of personal information to an unauthorized person. The California bill defines personal information as a person's first name or first initial and last name, in combination with any of the following:

- Social Security number
- Driver's license number
- Account number, debit or credit card number, plus whatever password or security code allows access to the account

The bill also defines several kinds of notification as acceptable:

- Written notice
- Electronic notice
- Substitute notice if the cost of notification would exceed $250,000 or if more than 500,000 people have to be notified. Substitute notice includes

e-mail, conspicuous posting of the notice on the organization's Web page, or an announcement to statewide media.

The bill also states that organizations aren't required to disclose any breach of personal information if that disclosure would affect an ongoing criminal investigation.

This bill is important because it provides legal impetus to actually report a privacy breach, something that might not otherwise happen because corporations are notoriously reluctant to report serious intrusions. This bill also encourages companies to take better care of your private information to save themselves the embarrassment, loss of customer goodwill, and potential lawsuits that would result from an unauthorized disclosure of information.

If you happen to be one of the many millions of Americans who don't live in California, you might say, "Who cares?" Well, one reason is that the bill applies to companies that have California residents as customers, not just companies located in California. Thus, businesses outside California likely will be compelled to report disclosures of personal information.

A case in point is the ChoicePoint incident. In February 2005, the data aggregation company, which collects personal information such as credit card and Social Security numbers of millions of consumers, announced that scammers had defrauded the company into revealing the personal identity information of thousands of California residents. ChoicePoint, which is headquartered in Georgia, made the announcement because of SB 1386. However, investigators publicly questioned whether thieves had targeted only California residents, and 19 state Attorneys General demanded to know if information about residents from other states had been compromised. Under the pressure ChoicePoint admitted that information about consumers in other states had also been disclosed—more than 145,000 consumer profiles.

SB 1386 has been proposed as a model for a federal law that would apply to the entire country. The federal proposal, introduced by California Senator Dianne Feinstein, is known by its Senate Bill designation, S. 1350. You can read the text of the proposed legislation by going to http://thomas.loc.gov/home/search.html and searching for bill number S. 1350 in the 108th Congress.

continues . . .

A Personal Experience with Potential Identity Theft

In March 2005, I received a letter from Boston College, of which I'm an alumnus. Unlike the usual alumni mailings that ask for donations, this letter described a break-in to a computer that contained personal information—names; addresses; and telephone, credit card, and Social Security numbers—of approximately 120,000 alumni, including me.

According to the college, the intruder hadn't broken in to steal confidential information. BC's investigation concluded that the attacker had hijacked the computer as a launchpad to attack other targets.

In addition to the letter notifying me of the breach, the college also included a fact sheet with instructions for placing a fraud alert with Equifax, Experian, and TransUnion, the three major credit bureaus. At first I thought I wouldn't bother, because I believed BC was right that the attacker hadn't attempted to steal any data. However, since I'd recently completed this chapter about identity theft, I decided it couldn't hurt.

I chose Experian at random as the first call. (You can find the 800 numbers for all three credit bureaus in the "Checklist" section.) The entire transaction was conducted via automated voice prompt; I never heard an option to speak with a human. However, the automated system was easy to navigate. After requesting to add a temporary fraud alert, I used my phone's keypad to enter my Social Security number and zip code. I also chose the option to have credit card companies call me for confirmation before any new accounts are opened in my name (I had to enter my phone number to do this). The automated system then gave me a confirmation number (so be sure to have pen and paper ready if you go through this). Experian also gave me the option to share this alert with Equifax and TransUnion. I accepted the option to save myself two additional phone calls and extra button-pressing. Several days later I received letters from all three credit bureaus confirming that the fraud alert had been put in place.

My next call was to order a copy of my credit report. You can request a credit report from any of the credit bureaus. You can also go to a special Web site to order it online (www.annualcreditreport.com), or you can call 877-322-8228. Again I had to navigate an automated voice system. This system was a bit trickier than Experian's because it needed more information, including my address and birth date. The system also had incorrectly listed my address, and getting it corrected took a bit of doing. The system can respond to either keypad or voice commands, but it took several tries to finally get it right.

Next I contacted the Social Security Administration (SSA). However, the representative I spoke with said the administration has no way of telling if someone is misusing my Social Security number. He suggested that I take the steps previously described. He also said that if my Social Security number was in fact being abused, I should take documentation of the abuse to a local SSA branch, which would review the case to see if it warranted issuing a new number.

My last call was to my local police department. I felt a little uncertain about making this call, because I was pretty sure that nothing had been stolen, but I figured it couldn't hurt. I used the non-emergency number, but it was immediately clear that identity theft is not a priority for the Oakland PD. The non-emergency number routes you to yet another automated voice system, and none of the selections offered by the message system (check someone's bail status, report juvenile delinquency, and so on) was even remotely related. Eventually I navigated my way to an answering machine for my precinct's patrol desk. I left a message, but my call was never returned. (I don't blame them for not calling back; after all, no crime had been committed as far as I could tell.)

Experts say that getting a police report is essential for resolving cases of identity theft, but I've also heard this can be one of the most difficult requirements to meet because local police departments simply don't know what to make of such requests. My suggestion is that if you need to fill out a report, visit the station in person to ensure that you get to speak to an actual human (the automated phone system is a brick wall). This way, you can explain that the report is necessary to satisfy your bank or credit card company, and you can reassure the officer that you don't expect the local police to conduct the investigation.

Chapter 3

Firewalls

A firewall is a piece of software or hardware that manages Internet communications to and from your computer. It monitors the programs and applications that try to initiate communications with your computer from the Internet, and it controls which programs on your computer are allowed to transmit information to the Internet.

Your mother probably told you never to talk to strangers, and for good reason—there are lots of people out there you can't trust. Her advice also applies on the Internet. A properly configured firewall is basically a computerized version of your mother's instructions. The Internet is full of computers you can't trust, and a firewall can keep your computer from engaging in conversations with strangers. In other words, it can prevent unsolicited connections from computers on the Internet. This is separate from a solicited connection, such as when you launch a Web browser and type a specific URL into the address field, or when you check your e-mail. You initiate the connection with another computer, and that computer then participates in an exchange of information. A firewall's primary role is to alert you to unsolicited connection attempts and block them.

Firewalls are strong protection against several kinds of threats, such as attackers who scan the Internet looking for potential victims, and automated worms. As you learned in Chapter 1, "Understanding Internet Risk," worms are programs that may try to exploit software flaws to gain access to, and control over, as many computers as possible. Firewalls are effective at detecting some kinds of worms that rely on unsolicited connections, in which a machine you didn't contact tries to get access to your computer.

The following section digs a little deeper into how your computer talks to other computers on the Internet. This will give you a better understanding of just how a firewall does what it does, and why it's a valuable tool for anyone who uses the Internet. Subsequent sections examine two firewalls you can get for free, as well as review the reasons for paying for software protection. This chapter focuses exclusively on software firewalls (that is, firewalls you install on your hard drive just like any other software application). Hardware firewalls perform the same kinds of functions but are deployed on a separate device that sits between your computer and your Internet connection. Many of the consumer routers that allow multiple computers to share one Internet connection include a firewall.

3.1 Packets, Protocols, and Ports

The more I learn about the Internet, the more amazed I am that it actually works. Many brilliant minds have worked hard to disguise the Internet's organic complexity behind friendly application front ends. This section peels back one or two layers of that disguise to help you better appreciate how the Internet works and why control software such as a firewall is essential. If you aren't at all curious about how the Internet works, you can skip the following section. If you do read it, at the very least you'll be able to impress your non-geek friends by discoursing wisely on the Internet's technological underpinnings.

The basic unit of Internet communication is called a packet. Every Web page you see, e-mail you receive, or file you download is first chopped into small packets, each of which is delivered individually to your computer. Your computer reassembles these packets into a coherent structure to display to you.

The ways in which packets are constructed, addressed, and routed through the Internet are governed by a set of rules that provide a common framework for every computer to follow. These rules are called protocols. Protocols are overseen by a variety of governing bodies, such as the Internet Engineering Task Force (IETF, www.ietf.org) and the IEEE (Institute of Electrical and Electronics Engineers, www.ieee.org).

Every protocol or application uses ports to connect to individual computers. Ports are the access ways through which information enters and leaves your computer. There are 65,535 possible ports in use today, and some applications use specific ports. For instance, HTTP (Web) traffic uses ports 80 and 8080, and

HTTPS (encrypted Web traffic) uses port 443. File-sharing programs and instant-messaging systems use a variety of ports; many of these programs are instructed to use whatever ports are available.

Because applications use ports to access computers, one job of the firewall is to monitor which ports are allowed to communicate with the PC. Ports are logical, not physical, so don't bother looking for 65,535 tiny doors on the backside of your machine.

IP and TCP

The cornerstone protocols for the Internet are IP (Internet Protocol) and TCP (Transmission Control Protocol). You may have heard of IP in reference to Voice over IP (VoIP), a new technology that allows you to make phone calls over the Internet.

IP describes how to send packets from one computer to another. Each computer on the Internet has an address (an IP address). This address is made up of four groups of up to three numbers, each separated by a period, or dot. IP addresses are sometimes called "dotted quads." Here's an example of an IP address: 192.101.432.156.

If you use a dial-up modem to access the Internet, your service provider assigns your computer a new IP address each time you access the Internet. The same thing happens with cable modems and DSL (Digital Subscriber Line) connections, except that the IP address stays with you as long as you don't log off or power down your computer. Many people who use cable modems or DSL connections leave the Internet on for days or weeks at a time.

While it's convenient to have instant Internet access, a long-term IP address can become a risk.

That's because computer criminals are constantly scanning the Internet using special software that looks for machines that may be easy to break into. Scanning wide swaths of the Internet takes time, and these tools note potentially vulnerable IP addresses that an intruder can go back to later. If your IP address is persistent, that intruder will have an easier time finding you again. For example, the creator of the Blaster.B worm used pre-infected machines as command stations to launch more attacks. He knew these command machines would be available weeks after he had broken into them because they were connected to cable modems, so the IP addresses were the same. (High-speed connections are also popular with Internet criminals because they can spew attacks more quickly than dial-up connections.)

Every Internet user should have a firewall because every Internet user has an address—it's akin to putting a lock on your door. At this point, the Internet is full of unlocked doors, and criminals have their pick of targets. By using a properly configured firewall, you remove yourself from the pool of easy targets. This illustrates an important point about computer security: your security system doesn't have to be perfect—it just has to be better than your neighbors'. If you lock your doors at night and your neighbors don't, the smart criminal will go after the easier targets.

As mentioned, when one computer sends information to another, it breaks that information into packets. Each packet is stamped with the sending computer's IP address (the source address) and the recipient's IP address (the destination address). Each packet also contains a portion of the total information to be sent to the destination (this chunk of information is called the payload). The sender transmits its packets to a local router. A router is a network computer whose job is to pass packets from one place to another. Routers maintain records called tables that describe the best pathways to various destinations on the network. Packets may travel through numerous routers before reaching the recipient computer.

IP is known as a "best effort" protocol. The protocol has no mechanism to determine whether the packets have arrived at their destination. The IP protocol simply tosses its packets onto the network and hopes they make it.

To add more control to the sending and receiving of messages, TCP was developed. TCP adds sequence numbers to a transmission so that a recipient machine knows how many packets to expect (for instance, this is packet number 5 out of an expected eight packets). TCP also provides mechanisms to ensure that all the packets in a transmission have arrived, and if they haven't, to resend missing packets. Based on the routing decisions made along the journey, packet 5 might arrive before packet 4. The recipient machine holds the packets until they've all arrived and then reassembles them in the proper order and passes them to other layers of the computer for processing.

TCP is known as a stateful protocol because it monitors the state of the transmission. Rather than flinging packets onto the Internet, TCP contacts the recipient machine and monitors the transmission to make sure all the packets have arrived. If not, the recipient machine can request that missing packets be re-sent.

HTTP and HTML

This next set of protocols are technically not Internet protocols. They are World Wide Web protocols. While many people speak of the Web and the Internet interchangeably, they are discrete entities. What's the difference? The Internet is a mechanism for connecting computers across a physical distance. The World Wide Web is a formalized way of presenting information and navigating through information repositories (such as Web sites). The Web also rides on top of the Internet; that is, the protocols used by the Web are transported from place to place by protocols including TCP and IP.

Tim Berners-Lee, a British physicist, invented the World Wide Web by creating Hypertext Markup Language (HTML) and Hypertext Transport Protocol (HTTP). HTML is the language for creating Web pages. HTTP is the mechanism for transporting HTML.

HTML instructs Web browsers how to present text and gives users the ability to click links embedded within text. You can see HTML source code on a Web page in the Internet Explorer browser by opening the View menu at the top of the page and choosing Source.

Berners-Lee's most significant contribution is that instead of patenting his idea, he made it freely available to anyone who wanted it. This led to a blossoming of creativity that has made the Web such a pervasive and information-rich medium.

Another milestone in the development of the World Wide Web was the creation of the Netscape Navigator Web browser. Written by Marc Andreessen and Jim Clark, the Netscape browser created a common environment for viewing Web pages. Today Web browsers have become the most widely used mechanism through which people experience the World Wide Web and the Internet.

3.2 What Firewalls Can Do

We started this chapter comparing firewalls to motherly advice not to talk to strangers. Now we'll talk more about how firewalls can protect you, as well as examine their limitations.

Regulate Inbound and Outbound Connections

A firewall's primary function is to regulate inbound and outbound connections to your computer. It does this by examining each application or protocol that tries to open a port on your computer. You may not be aware of it, but when you are on the Internet, programs are knocking on your door constantly. If you have a firewall installed, you can set it to alert you every time a program tries to establish a connection with your computer. Often these programs are port scanners, which are software tools that scan target machines, looking for open ports they can use to access your computer.

It's also important for a firewall to be able to stop your computer from talking to the Internet. If you have a Trojan horse, spyware, or other piece of malware on your PC, a firewall can prevent it from establishing outbound connections to other computers. This is necessary because it prevents your computer from becoming a source of attacks against other computers, from allowing spyware to report on your activities, or from letting malware get new orders from or be upgraded by a control system.

A good firewall should be able to do the following:

- Make your PC invisible. Remember that your computer has 65,535 ports, all of which can be used to initiate a connection with another computer on the Internet. While it's important to allow your computer to use ports associated with popular applications such as the Web, e-mail, and instant messaging, there's no reason that unknown computers on the Internet should be trying to access your machine via uncommon ports. One way that Internet criminals break into computers is by attempting to open connections on every possible port on a target system. They do this by sending TCP/IP requests; if the target computer responds to a particular request, the attacker has found a potential entrance into your computer.

  Thus, a good firewall does not respond to TCP/IP requests to ports that aren't used for common Internet use. By not responding, your computer in effect becomes invisible. This is often referred to as putting a computer into stealth mode.

- Alert you to suspicious behavior. A firewall should be able to tell you when a program or connection is attempting to do something unwanted, such as download software or run a program like ActiveX. (ActiveX is a Microsoft technology that can execute programs downloaded from Internet Explorer. Some ActiveX programs are benign, but attackers also exploit ActiveX to insert malware onto users' computers. You can learn more about ActiveX in Chapter 5, "Getting Rid of Unwanted Guests, Part 2: Spyware, Adware, and Trojan Horses.") However, this feature has drawbacks as well. While I am comfortable saying "yes" to connection requests from trusted Web sites, many warning messages are difficult to understand. Some firewalls, such as

Zone Alarm Pro, can provide additional information about warnings to help you decide whether to allow an action or connection.

- Block outbound connections you didn't initiate. As mentioned, malware on your computer may attempt to contact other machines on the Internet. If you haven't explicitly launched a program, a good firewall informs you when a program on your computer is trying to access the Internet on its own.

Security Settings

Most firewalls let you adjust their security settings. For example, Norton Internet Security includes a slider bar that has Low, Medium, and High levels, as shown in Figure 3.1. These settings adjust the level of protection the firewall provides. Generally speaking, the higher the setting, the greater the protection.

Figure 3.1 Norton Internet Security firewall settings.

However, higher settings also have the potential to disrupt your Internet usage. Hyper-vigilant firewalls may interrupt Web surfing, file downloads, and other processes that you regard as normal but the firewall mistrusts. At the very least you may spend more time clicking the Allow button to let interrupted processes continue.

One way to decide which level is best for you is to start with the highest setting and see how much disruption it causes. You can gradually adjust downward until you reach a level you are comfortable with. Remember to keep in mind the trade-offs: Lower security generally improves ease of use but also increases your exposure to attack or infiltration. You'll have to find the balance that's right for you.

Advanced users may also want to tinker with the guts of the firewall, playing with rules that involve more steps than sliding a bar from High to Low, such as blocking specific ports or applications.

Your firewall also keeps track of all the machines it communicates with. This list is called the firewall log. This log makes little sense unless you have some experience with computer networking. But if you're interested in seeing what an IP address looks like, what ports your computer is using, and the IP addresses of the places you connect to, you should take a look at the log. Windows XP Service Pack 2 includes a built-in firewall. Its default file destination for the logs is C:WINDOWS/pfirewall, as shown in Figure 3.2, but you can have the file written anywhere you like. Note that this log function works only for the Windows Firewall. Third-party firewall products create their own logs, which you should be able to find through the user interface.

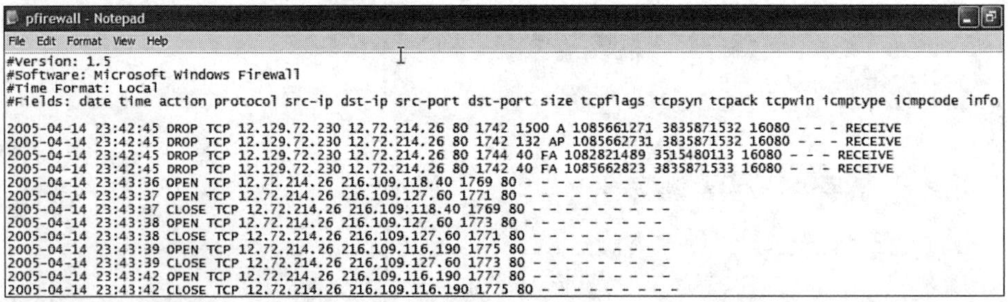

Figure 3.2 The firewall log.

The log format includes the date and time of each action, a description of the action (for example, opening a connection to another computer), the protocol

(TCP and so on), the source and destination IP addresses, the source and destination ports, and information about the individual packets that make up Internet communications.

3.3 What Firewalls Can't Do

Firewalls are an important component for home security, but they do have limits. Many Internet attacks use ports and applications that are commonly allowed to pass through the firewall, including the Web and e-mail. Thus, if your firewall allows Web and e-mail traffic (and if it doesn't, there's really not much point in being on the Internet), the firewall likely won't stop attacks that use these entrances.

For instance, the most popular infection vector for viruses and worms is an attachment to an e-mail. As long as your firewall is configured to allow e-mail, it is helpless to stop viruses that arrive as e-mail attachments.

The same is also somewhat true for the Web. Many Web pages use a variety of software programs, such as cookies, ActiveX, and Java, to make your browsing experience faster and more visually interesting. However, all these programs can be misused by attackers, who embed malware in Web sites. This malware downloads itself onto your computer when you surf to that site (this is sometimes called a drive-by download).

Last, firewalls do only what you tell them to do. If a firewall asks you whether you want to allow a specific program to run, and you say yes, if that program turns out to be malicious, you can't blame the firewall. Deciding whether to allow a connection is probably one of the most difficult parts of computer security for home users.

There are a couple of ways to deal with alerts you don't understand. If you are on a reputable site, such as a well-known e-commerce, ISP, or banking site, you likely can allow programs to execute without being concerned. For instance, whenever I attach a file to an e-mail using Yahoo! Mail, my firewall warns me that an ActiveX program wants to execute. I always click Allow because I trust Yahoo!. If you like to be more cautious, another option is to deny the action. The risk here is that the application or transaction may not function, in which case you have to start over.

Another option is to copy the name of the program, application, or service that is trying to establish a connection and then paste it into the search field of your favorite search engine. The results may help you decide whether to allow the connection.

For more complete protection, firewall software should be used in conjunction with anti-virus (AV) and anti-spyware software, both of which are covered in this book.

3.4 Free Firewalls

A tight budget is not an excuse for poor computer security. This section looks at two firewalls you can download at no cost. While these two are the best known, Table 3.2 lists other free firewalls.

Windows XP Service Pack 2

The Microsoft Corporation is being punished by its own success. Because it is the most widely installed PC operating system in the world, it is also the most widely targeted by Internet criminals. Malware writers and malicious hackers routinely discover new flaws in the Windows operating system and other Microsoft applications and use those flaws to hijack PCs, steal or corrupt data, and otherwise perpetrate Internet crime.

The most well-known viruses and worms of the past few years (Blaster, Slammer, MyDoom, Code Red, Nimda, and so on) all have targeted Windows, Internet Explorer, or other Microsoft applications. While some people say that any publicity is good publicity, the repeated exploitation of Microsoft products has garnered harsh criticism for the company and has prompted many corporate customers to consider alternatives such as Linux. (Consumers should strongly consider switching to a Mac, which has considerably fewer security issues. Of course, if the Mac gets as popular as Windows PCs, I can guarantee you Internet criminals will find ways to exploit it. At this point, however, the Mac platform is the safest bet for consumers.)

Microsoft has responded by attempting to write more-secure code and by including security features in its products. On the consumer front, its biggest step toward a more secure computing environment is Windows XP Service Pack 2 (SP2), the latest upgrade of the Microsoft operating system. The SP2 upgrade is available for free (assuming that you've already purchased XP—those running Windows 98, Windows 2000, Windows Me, or, God help you, Windows 95, are out of luck).

You can download SP2 from Windows Update (but it's a large file, so be sure to set aside at least half an hour if you are on a dial-up connection), or you can order the upgrade on a CD-ROM from www.microsoft.com/windowsxp/sp2/default.mspx.

SP2 includes the Windows Security Center, shown in Figure 3.3, which monitors basic security information about your PC. It uses simple shield icons in green, yellow, and red to indicate your computer's security status. After you install the software, you can find Security Center by opening Control Panel. Security Center lets you control three SP2 security features: Windows Firewall, Automatic Updates, and Virus Protection.

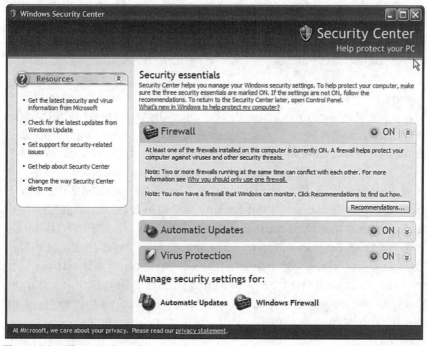

Figure 3.3   The Windows Security Center.

Windows Firewall

SP2 includes free firewall software designed specifically for Windows XP. It blocks unsolicited inbound connection attempts from computers or programs on the Internet. Worms, viruses, and intruders attempt to connect to your firewall using a variety of ports and protocols. The Windows Firewall can block those connection attempts. However, as with most firewalls, you have to tell the Windows Firewall which connections you want to accept and which you want to block. When you click Yes to allow a connection, you create exceptions to the firewall rules; once you create an exception, the firewall will not block future programs on the exceptions list.

Some programs require exceptions to function properly; for instance, instant messaging, file sharing, and online gaming usually use a variety of ports. However, the more exceptions you create, the more ports you leave open. As mentioned, Internet criminals continuously scan the Internet for open ports that will allow them to connect to your machine. Therefore, it's in your best interests to limit the number of exceptions you create.

Windows Firewall also includes a log. This log records all the firewall activity, including the connections it blocked and allowed. You don't need to spend much time puzzling over logs, but they can provide helpful clues if you see particular programs acting strangely or if you suspect you may have been infected by malware.

You have to explicitly activate the log function because it is not activated by default. To do so, open the Windows Firewall and click the Advanced tab. Under the listing for Security Logging, you can select one of two options: Log dropped packets, which lists all the connection attempts the firewall blocked, or Log successful connections, which lists all the connections the firewall allowed.

Of course, while the notion of a free firewall is a good step, the SP2 firewall only protects against unauthorized inbound connections. While unsolicited inbound connections tend to be the most dangerous, the Windows Firewall does only half the job, because it doesn't stop existing malware on your PC from making outbound connections. Thus, you may want to consider other alternatives. Most commercial firewalls (and the free ZoneAlarm firewall, described later) monitor both inbound and outbound connections. With that said, if you don't want to bother buying or downloading another firewall, at the very least you should take advantage of the Windows Firewall.

If you have another firewall installed, or if you prefer to use a different firewall, you won't be doubly protected by using a third-party firewall at the same time as the Windows Firewall. In fact, running two or more firewalls on the same machine simultaneously may disrupt your Internet usage. To disable the Internet firewall, click the Windows Firewall icon at the bottom of the Security Center page. A pop-up window appears; simply click the Off button. Some third-party firewalls can also turn off the Windows Firewall during installation.

For a list of frequently asked questions (FAQs) about using Microsoft's Internet firewall, go to www.microsoft.com/athome/security/protect/firewall.mspx.

For more information about configuring the Windows Firewall, see Chapter 7, "Securing Windows."

Automatic Updates

Malicious hackers are constantly uncovering new bugs in computer systems, especially in Microsoft products. Each time a new bug is found, Microsoft creates a fix or patch to prevent that bug from being exploited by a worm or virus. If you enable Automatic Updates, Microsoft sends these fixes or patches to your computer when they become available. Automatic Updates is highly recommended because of the speed with which new exploits emerge. If you are less than diligent about retrieving operating system patches or updating AV software, the Automatic Updates feature can go a long way toward locking out malicious users without significant effort on your part. Chapter 7 discusses patches and fixes.

Virus Protection

SP2 doesn't protect you from viruses, but it does monitor the status of third-party AV software. The Virus Protection feature tells you whether your AV software is on and whether it is up to date. Of course, the AV software program should also be able to alert you if it's out of date, but it can't hurt to be reminded again.

Microsoft does not support all AV software programs. You can find out if your AV software is supported by surfing to www.microsoft.com/security/partners/antivirus.asp. A partial list of supported AV programs includes Symantec, Trend Micro, Computer Associates, GFI, F-Secure, Sophos, Kaspersky, McAfee, and Panda Software.

Security Center also includes an Internet Options feature that lets you create lists of trusted and restricted Web sites, adjust online privacy settings, and enable other security settings. Chapter 7 covers these options.

Zone Labs' ZoneAlarm

Zone Labs is a computer security company (now owned by CheckPoint Software Technologies, a major provider of security products to businesses). The company makes a free Internet firewall called Zone Alarm, which is available for download at its Web site (www.zonelabs.com).

The free ZoneAlarm firewall is a fairly comprehensive piece of software, considering it doesn't cost you a thing. The ZoneAlarm firewall performs five major functions: Firewall, Program Control, Anti-Virus Monitoring, E-Mail Protection, and Alerts and Logs.

Firewall

The software firewall monitors inbound connections to help protect you from would-be intruders. The firewall includes two security zones that allow you to adjust the security settings. The Internet Zone deals with all the computers on the Internet. The Trusted Zone creates settings for computers you trust, such as those on a home network with which you share files.

Program Control

ZoneAlarm monitors the programs on your computer that request Internet connections. This outbound protection mechanism helps prevent Trojan horses, spyware, and other malware that may be on your machine from reaching out to the Internet. After you install the software, ZoneAlarm alerts you each time a program wants to connect to the Internet. As you allow trusted programs, such as Web browsers, chat programs, or e-mail, the firewall automatically allows those programs to operate.

Anti-Virus Monitoring

While the free firewall doesn't actually perform virus checking, it does monitor AV software. It alerts you if your software is out of date or turned off. However, it performs these functions for only three AV programs: Symantec's Norton AntiVirus, McAfee's Viruscan, and Computer Associates' EZ Antivirus. Note that most AV programs also tell you if your AV software is out of date.

E-Mail Protection

This feature quarantines file attachments that arrive via e-mail. E-mail attachments are the primary method of spreading viruses and worms. However, the free version of ZoneAlarm quarantines only attachments of the .vbs type. (VBS stands for Visual Basic Script, a computer language that used to be very popular among virus writers but that has fallen somewhat out of use these days.)

Alerts and Logs

This feature performs two functions. Alerts are pop-up messages that require some kind of response from you. These pop-up messages address both information alerts (a notification that something has happened) and program alerts (a program is attempting to perform a function).

You can select to show all alerts or just the program alerts. You may want to show all the alerts for the first few days you use the software. This gives you a better understanding of what's going on when you use the Internet. However, you may find yourself besieged by pop-up messages, in which case you can switch to the program alerts setting, which alerts you to only potentially harmful activities.

Logs are records of the firewall's activities, including traffic that the software has blocked. You can view your logs by clicking the Log Viewer tab in the Alerts & Logs section. You can also click a specific log entry to get more information about the event.

3.5 Firewalls You Can Buy

The previous section spent a lot of time looking at two free firewalls. Both are pretty good, and you can find even more firewalls by searching for "free personal firewalls." When you compare a free firewall to a $50 firewall, is there any good reason to pay for one? If you are just talking about firewalls, I'd have a hard time saying yes.

However, there is one excellent reason to buy a firewall: Many are bundled with other essential Internet security products, such anti-virus software, spam protection, and spyware detection. Firewalls won't stop e-mail viruses or spam, so getting them bundled with other products makes them worth the money. Commercial firewalls also offer more features and options than the freeware versions, such as Web privacy, pop-up blocking, and the ability to spot and block known worms.

For instance, the ZoneAlarm Security Suite includes a firewall, AV software, and other features such as protection from e-mail and instant messaging fraud, Web privacy protection, and other features not found in the free version.

Symantec's Norton Internet Security is another product bundle that includes a firewall, AV software, anti-spyware software, and other essential products, including protection against phishing emails along with anti-spam software and parental control software to protect and monitor your children while they're online.

Trend Micro's PC-cillin Internet Security product also bundles a personal firewall, AV software, anti-spam software, anti-spyware software, and protection from phishing attacks.

McAfee's Internet Security Suite packages a personal firewall, AV software, spyware detection and removal, spam protection, and Web privacy software into a single product.

Table 3.1 lists the most popular personal firewall products on the market today. Prices range from $39.95 to $79.95 (as of mid-2005), but special offers and rebates may affect the final cost. Table 3.2 lists free firewalls.

Table 3.1

Leading Personal Firewall Products			
Product	**Vendor**	**Web Site**	**Features**
Black ICE PC Protection	Internet Security Systems	www.blackICE.iss.net	Firewall, intrusion detection, and more
eTrust EZ Armor	Computer Associates	www.ca.com or www.my-etrust.com	Firewall, AV, and more
F-Secure Internet Security	F-Secure	www.f-secure.com	Firewall, AV, anti-spyware, and more
Internet Security Suite	McAfee	www.mcafee.com	Firewall, AV, anti-spam, anti-spyware, and more
Kaspersky Personal Security Suite	Kaspersky Lab	www.kaspersky.com	Firewall, AV, anti-spam, anti-spyware, and more
Norton Internet Security	Symantec	www.symantec.com	Firewall, AV, anti-spyware, anti-spam, and more
Panda Platinum Internet Security	Panda Software	www.pandasoftware.com	Firewall, AV, anti-spam, anti-spyware, and more
PC-cillin Internet Security	Trend Micro	www.trendmicro.com	Firewall, AV, anti-spam, anti-spyware, and more
Sygate Personal Firewall Pro	Sygate Technologies	www.sygate.com	Firewall, intrusion detection, and more
ZoneAlarm Security Suite	ZoneLabs	www.zonelabs.com	Firewall, AV, e-mail protection, and more

Table 3.2

Free Firewalls		
Product	Vendor	Web Site
Kerio Personal Firewall	Kerio Technologies	www.kerio.com
Sygate Personal Firewall Standard	Sygate Technologies	http://smb.sygate.com/products/spf_standard.htm
Windows XP Service Pack 2	Microsoft	www.microsoft.com/windowsxp/sp2/default.mspx
ZoneAlarm	ZoneLabs	www.zonelabs.com

How Should You Choose?

The best resources for helping you choose a firewall product are the Internet and people you know. The Internet is crawling with reviews, opinions, and information on security products. The simplest method is to enter the name of a particular product into a search engine and fire away. You may have to sort through a lot of links to the company that sells the product, but you're likely to come across other interesting links.

For a more targeted search, check out online resources such as CNET.com. This Web site contains reviews of numerous computer security products, including personal firewalls. Publications such as *PC Magazine* and *PC World* also let you search their Web sites for product reviews.

A second option is to try several yourself. Most firewalls can be downloaded from the Internet, and they come with a trial period, usually between 30 and 90 days. You can use magazine reviews and your friends' advice to whittle down the list to two or three contenders, and then give each of them a test run.

Use the test period to find out which product feels best to you. Which has the most bang for your buck? Which has the cleanest or most appealing user interface? Which do you feel most comfortable tinkering with? Which firewall does the best job with alerts? Which company provides the best technical support? Which firewall makes you feel safest? Which has the best colors? Whatever your particular criteria, you can test to your heart's content. In fact, if you're willing to put up with long download times, you probably can get a year's worth of free coverage by simply hopping from trial version to trial version.

3.6 Testing Firewalls

How do you know if your firewall is working? One way to find out is to test it. Many testing sites available on the Internet scan your computer and report on the results. Here are a few good sites to help you see just how your computer looks from the outside in.

ShieldsUP! (www.grc.com)

This site, run by security guru Steve Gibson, has been scanning users' PCs for years (with the users' permission, of course). It's a great way to check out a few common vulnerabilities, such as Windows file sharing via NetBIOS, and common ports that may open (and thus become accessible to bad guys). The results are clear and easy to understand. The site also includes links to more information about personal firewalls and computer security.

The site offers several tests. Two of them are particularly useful for home users. The first is called Common Ports and checks 26 often-used ports that may open (and thus become accessible to bad guys). The second test is called Service Ports and checks 1,056 ports. It's a more comprehensive test and takes a bit longer.

Other testing sites may perform similar functions, but no one does it with Gibson's gusto and enthusiasm. If you're testing your firewall to see how it stands up to potential Internet intruders, this should be your first stop.

Symantec Security Check (www.symantec.com/homecomputing/)

Symantec Security Check scans your computer for a variety of potential vulnerabilities, including ports that may respond to unsolicited requests, the presence of Trojan horse programs, and whether you are running anti-virus software. The test results are understandable (although much drier than Gibson's), and detailed results are available for the Hacker Test (which shows ports that do or don't respond to connection requests). The check requires an ActiveX download to operate.

McAfee MySecurityStatus (http://us.mcafee.com/MySecurityStatus/)

Like Symantec Security Check, MySecurityStatus requires an ActiveX download to check the status of your personal firewall and anti-virus software.

PivX PreView (www.pivx.com/preview)

PreView is a free, downloadable security tool from a company called PivX. The tool gives your computer a security grade based on four categories: Threat Center, Security Software, Patches/HotFixes, and Firewall Protection. PreView analyzes your computer to calculate a security score using the four categories. It's a simple way to communicate how vulnerable your computer is to attack. However, a significant portion of your score is based on whether you've purchased another PivX product, so take the score with a grain of salt.

The tool has a variety of functions (which are described in more detail in Chapter 7), one of which is to conduct a basic probe of your firewall. It scans your machine from the Internet to see what ports are open and are responding to unsolicited requests.

To launch the scan, click the Firewall Protection icon. Before the scan launches, you have to accept the terms under which the scan is conducted. The terms basically want to verify that you are the owner of the computer and are authorized to make such a request. Your firewall may alert you that the PreView executable is attempting to contact the Internet when you launch the scan. This is OK, so you should permit the action.

The scan checks 16 common ports, including port 80 (for the Web) and port 25 (for SMTP, a protocol for sending e-mail). The report tells you the status of each of the ports (open or closed) and the common purpose of each port. If your firewall is running in Stealth mode, you should receive a high grade. Remember that a closed port is ideal. This doesn't mean your Web browser won't connect to the Web; it simply means that your firewall won't respond to unsolicited attempts to open a communications channel.

AuditMyPC (www.auditmypc.com)

This site checks for available ports on your machine. It can also scan for spyware and Web browser vulnerabilities. Test results aren't quite as informative as the ones just mentioned, but the site does allow you to scan all 65,535 ports rather than just the handful most commonly abused by intruders. It also allows you to test selected ports.

3.7 Checklist

Use this checklist as a quick-reference guide to the material covered in this chapter.

Do

- Install firewall software on your computer and use the "stealth" setting.
- Download Windows XP Service Pack 2 or order a CD at www.microsoft.com/windowsxp/sp2/default.mspx.
- Strongly consider using a firewall that includes anti-virus, anti-spyware and other capabilities.
- Test your firewall using one or more of the sites listed in the section "Testing Firewalls."
- Check with your firewall provider regularly for software updates.
- Back up your important files regularly.

Don't

- Use the Internet without a firewall.
- Believe that a firewall will protect you from all Internet risks.

3.8 Helpful Resources

This section presents additional resources to help you learn more.

RTFM. This is short for "Read the f****** manual." Many questions can be answered by the user guides shipped with the product or at online FAQ sites. If you post basic questions at online help sites, though, don't be surprised if you get this reply.

The Web site www.firewallguide.com is a great resource when you're shopping for security software and hardware. It has tons of information on firewalls and other solutions, including anti-virus and anti-spyware tools. The site also aggregates articles from popular computer magazines, including reviews and comparisons of home security products.

Secrets and Lies: Digital Security in a Networked World by Bruce Schneier. This book provides a great overview of computer security, including firewalls, although it is not a how-to guide. It also talks about the human weaknesses at the heart of every security system (including the security professional's perpetual lament that the world's best security software is helpless in the face of people who click attachments). It presents complex topics with humor and clarity.

Chapter 4

Getting Rid of Unwanted Guests, Part 1: Viruses and Worms

Throughout this book we use the term *malware*. It's a general term that describes any piece of software intentionally created to harm a computer system. Malware encompasses a variety of malicious software, including viruses, worms, Trojan horses, and some high-risk spyware and adware.

This chapter examines the reasons behind the incredible rise of malware. It also discusses two specific kinds of malware: viruses and worms. We'll describe how they can get on to your computer, and steps you can take to protect yourself. We'll also look at the strengths and weaknesses of anti-virus software and discuss how you can block and/or remove viruses and worms.

4.1 The Rise of Malware

Malware has flourished for several reasons. First is computers' growing ability to communicate. In the old days (the late 1980s), malware traveled on floppy disks; to catch a virus, you had to put an infected disk into your computer. As the Internet grew, malware hitched a ride on various communications mechanisms. Today malware spreads via e-mail and instant messaging, various Internet protocols, and the World Wide Web.

The second reason malware has flourished is because of the increasing homogenization of our computing environments. Malware written for one operating system or chip platform can't function on others. In the early days this incompatibility acted as a barrier to infection, because back then computers ran on a variety of operating systems. Today, however, for the most part that variety has been whittled to two: Microsoft Windows and UNIX (including variants such as Linux). On top of that are common applications such as the Microsoft Office suite and Web browsers that work on multiple operating systems. Malware takes advantage of security weaknesses in these operating systems and application software and uses those weaknesses as a means of infecting the computer system. When you combine a homogenous computing environment with a multiplicity of network-based infection vectors, the result is widespread outbreaks that ravage home and corporate computers and the Internet alike.

The third reason malware has flourished is that traditional malware defense tools are reactive. Anti-virus and anti-spyware software is most effective against known attacks. However, if a new piece of malware emerges, there's a window of opportunity for the malware to spread while the security research community analyzes the attack, cooks up a remedy, and gets it distributed. The bad guys have the initiative, and they use it to their advantage. Firewalls can block access to unusual communication channels, but a large portion of Internet users either don't have a firewall or don't have it properly configured. Attackers also use common channels such as the Web or e-mail to spread malware. Some technologies are being developed that can detect and block new and unknown attacks, but such technology is still a work in progress; it often causes problems with legitimate programs and applications.

The fourth and most troubling reason malware is flourishing is because of money. Criminal syndicates and disreputable business organizations alike earn profits by writing programs you may not want on your computer. Previously, it was assumed that most malware writers were motivated by antisocial behavior; they wrote malicious programs to get peer approval from other like-minded miscreants or to stroke their own egos. A widespread malware outbreak garners the same kind of attention in the computer underground as a hit record does for a rock star or a best seller does for a novelist. (If you're interested in learning more about this topic, check out research by Sarah Gordon at www.badguys.org/papers.htm.)

But the injection of money into the equation changes the picture. Malware writers who operate for money don't want to make a big splash. They create silent or stealthy programs that infiltrate machines and remain there for as long as possible. Malware that gets press coverage is also malware that gets hunted down and removed. Malware that generates profits tries to remain hidden.

There are three ways to make money from writing and spreading malicious software. The first is espionage. Corporations and governments are perpetual targets of spies who are paid to steal state secrets or intellectual property. (For instance, in May 2005 it was reported that executives at three Israeli companies were arrested for hiring private investigators to spy on competitors. The private investigators used Trojan horse software to steal files and documents from infected computers. In an older case, hackers used the QAZ Worm to gain access to some of Microsoft's source code in 2000.) Malicious programs such as keystroke loggers and rootkits are part of the digital espionage tradecraft. (Rootkits are programs that reside deep inside a computer's operating system and give the attacker complete control over the computer. An attacker can return to a "rooted" computer at will and run whatever operations he or she chooses. Well-crafted rootkits can hide themselves from even seasoned computer administrators. Specialized forensic tools are required to discover and remove them.) While digital espionage has been around as long as computers have existed, rootkits aren't just tools of elite operatives; prebuilt rootkits can be had on the Internet for anyone interested in obtaining one.

Second, one can make money using malware by compromising and then renting large numbers of computers to spammers, scammers, and extortionists. Automated malware can discover, break into, and take over thousands of computers and assemble them into armies of slave machines that can be controlled remotely. These slave machines, sometimes called zombies or bots, can then be rented to others, who use them to send spam or launch denial-of-service (DoS) attacks. (A DoS attack floods a target site with so much traffic that legitimate users can't get access.) Home PCs with DSL or cable modems are popular targets because they are often unprotected, and their high-bandwidth Internet connections mean they can spew thousands of e-mail messages or spawn thousands of Web site connections per second. Spammers (and, more recently, phishers) can rent these bot networks to blast out the latest round of scam messages. Crime syndicates use bot networks to extort money from online gambling and porn sites by threatening to "DoS" them into bankruptcy. Security experts say that criminals may begin targeting more legitimate businesses as well.

The third way to profit from malware is through theft facilitated by spyware, or through advertising generated by high-risk adware. Spyware such as keystroke loggers can record sensitive information such as your online bank account ID and password and send it to an attacker who can then transfer money from your account. Adware programs facilitate delivery of advertising to your PC. In some cases, these programs may gather information from your computer, including information related to Internet browser usage or other computing habits, and relay this information back to a remote computer or other location in cyberspace. Companies pay adware firms to generate pop-up ads if you visit a competitor's site or visit sites related to the product or service they sell. Adware may also report your surfing activity to a home company that aggregates and resells the information as "consumer research." While programs like Trojan horses or viruses clearly are malicious (and in many cases illegal), adware occupies a gray area. Much of the adware circulating on the Internet is created by companies (as opposed to criminal syndicates or freelance programmers). These companies have a client list of businesses that use their services for advertising or market research and have their brand and reputation to protect, much like any other company. (Adware is discussed in more detail in Chapter 5, "Getting Rid of Unwanted Guests, Part 2: Spyware, Adware, and Trojan Horses.")

The point of all this is to demonstrate that malware is a serious problem that will continue to plague computer users until the end of time. Knowing the threat environment in which you operate means you can take steps to protect yourself. The goal here is not to make your computer invulnerable; that's impossible. However, the Internet is full of easy targets. Our goal is to make you a harder target.

4.2 Viruses and Worms

A virus is a program or code that replicates itself onto other files with which it comes into contact. A virus can infect another program, a boot sector, a partition sector, or a document that supports macros by inserting itself or attaching itself to that medium. Most viruses only replicate, but many can damage a computer system or a user's data as well (researchers call this the virus payload). Sometimes a virus requires human interaction to replicate, such as clicking a program that contains the virus or opening an infected file. Once activated, the virus can create and distribute copies of itself by infecting other programs or by spreading via communications mechanisms such as e-mail. Table 4.1 has more information about each virus type.

A worm is a program that facilitates the distribution of copies of itself, often without any human intervention. A worm may do damage and compromise the computer's security. It may arrive via exploitation of a system vulnerability, or

Table 4.1

Virus Terminology		
Type	**Examples**	**Description**
File infector virus	Cascade	File infector viruses attach themselves to programs, executable files, and scripts. If an infected file is run on a computer, the virus can spread to other programs.
Macro virus	Melissa, Concept	Macros are small programs that exist within larger applications such as Microsoft Word. Macros can be written to simplify common tasks. Macro viruses can copy themselves, delete or change documents, and perform other unwanted functions.
Boot sector virus	Michelangelo	The boot sector of a disk or hard drive tells the computer which programs to launch when the disk is read or how to start the operating system. Boot sector viruses are executed every time the disk is used or the computer starts.
Memory-resident virus	Jerusalem	A virus that stays in computer memory after the virus code is activated.
Polymorphic virus	Marburg, Zmist	A virus that can change its byte pattern when it replicates, thereby avoiding detection by simple string-scanning techniques.
Retro virus	Gobi	A virus that actively attacks an anti-virus program or programs in an effort to prevent detection.

when a user opens an infected e-mail or clicks an attachment. Unlike viruses, worms don't infect host files. Instead, they are built as self-sufficient programs that operate independently of other programs on the computer. In addition to using vehicles such as e-mail or instant messaging, some worms have a built-in engine that allows them to spread across the Internet and throughout local networks. Table 4.2 has more information about worms.

Today worms are increasingly designed to seek out and take advantage of specific flaws in popular operating systems or applications. These flaws, which are also called vulnerabilities, allow the worm to gain access to a computer, perform any task it's been assigned to complete, and then replicate itself to seek out other vulnerable computers. Sometimes software vendors are aware of the vulnerabilities, and they release software updates, also called security patches. Sometimes the software vendor doesn't know there's a problem until a new worm or other

Table 4.2

Worm Terminology		
Type	**Examples**	**Description**
Worm	Bugbear, Netsky, MyDoom	A worm is a program that makes and facilitates the distribution of copies of itself, such as from one disk drive to another or by copying itself using e-mail or another transport mechanism. The worm may do damage and compromise the computer's security. It may arrive via exploitation of a system vulnerability or when you click an infected e-mail.
Mailer and mass-mailing worm	LoveLetter (mass mailer), Happy99 (mailer)	Mailers and mass-mailing worms are a special class of computer worm that send themselves in an e-mail. Mass mailers send multiple copies of themselves, whereas mailers send themselves less frequently.
Blended threats	Nimda, Slammer, Blaster	Blended threats combine the characteristics of viruses, worms, and Trojan horses with software vulnerabilities to initiate, transmit, and spread an attack. Characteristics of blended threats include their ability to cause harm, propagate by multiple methods, and attack from multiple points, potentially spreading without human intervention and exploiting software vulnerabilities. By using multiple methods and techniques, blended threats can rapidly spread and cause extensive damage.

malware emerges and starts chewing its way through the Internet, at which point the vendor quickly rushes to release a fix. In either case, it's up to the end user (you) to find and apply the patches. One reason that worms are so successful, however, is that many users and businesses aren't very good about patching their computers. Chapter 7, "Securing Windows," goes into more detail about security patches.

As mentioned, worms frequently don't rely on human interaction. If the worm can establish a network connection with your computer, and your computer has the specific vulnerability that the worm is looking for, and you don't have any protection in place, the game is usually over.

What Can Worms and Viruses Do?

Both worms and viruses are created to carry a payload to the target computer. That payload is designed to perform a specific function, such as delete or change data, install software on your computer, or create a back door that an attacker can use later to get unauthorized access to your computer.

Worms and viruses both create problems for infected machines, but worms tend to cause more collateral damage because of the network traffic they generate when propagating across the Internet. For example, consider SQL Slammer, a fast-moving worm that targeted servers running a vulnerable version of Microsoft SQL Server 2000 software. (SQL stands for Structured Query Language, which is used in databases.) Launched in January 2003, the SQL Slammer worm rapidly took control of vulnerable machines and began to seek out new victims. At its peak propagation rate, the worm doubled the number of machines under its control every 8.5 seconds. The resulting flood of traffic generated by compromised computers brought the Internet to a standstill. Most of South Korea lost Internet access, Continental Airlines had to cancel flights out of its Newark hub, and numerous bank ATMs went out of service for hours.

Worms and viruses used to exist in discrete categories, but over the past few years they have begun to cross-pollinate to create blended threats with multiple ways to propagate themselves. For instance, many worms (called mass mailers) spread themselves via e-mail. Other worms use a variety of mechanisms to spread.

A good example is the Nimda worm, which emerged on September 18, 2001. This worm used five different methods to spread. The first was by scanning for Windows servers running a vulnerable version of IIS (IIS stands for Internet Information Server and is Microsoft's Web server software). Once it co-opted a server, it used that server as a launchpad to look for other vulnerable machines. It also spread through Outlook (Microsoft's e-mail software), mailing itself to addresses in the victim's address book. Nimda also installed itself on the computers of people who surfed to a Web server that had been infected with Nimda; it downloaded its code through Internet Explorer (Microsoft's browser). Nimda also spread through Windows File Sharing (Microsoft's mechanism for sharing files among computers) and through preexisting back doors that had been installed by two previous worms that had attacked Windows IIS servers.

4.3 Anti-Virus Software

You can protect your computer from becoming infected with viruses and worms in a variety of ways. The best protection against viruses and worms is anti-virus (AV) software. AV software can prevent viruses from being installed and can also detect, quarantine, and remove viruses and worms from your computer that may have slipped past your defenses.

Traditional AV software works by making a signature of each virus or piece of malware. A signature identifies a section of the code that appears only in the malware itself. Thus, a signature is like a fingerprint; it presents strong evidence of the program's identity. Every time your AV software scans an attachment in an e-mail or examines the files on your hard drive, it looks for the fingerprints of known viruses and worms.

What AV Software Can Do

AV software can protect you from known viruses that appear in several places: incoming and outgoing e-mail, instant messages, and your computer's hard drive. You should configure your AV software to automatically scan incoming and outgoing messages. If you use Web mail from service providers such as MSN, AOL, and Yahoo!, your service provider also scans your e-mail for viruses. (MSN uses virus scanning products from Trend Micro, Yahoo! uses Norton AntiVirus, and AOL uses McAfee.)

Most anti-virus products also come with a real-time scanner that checks your files every time you access them. You should also regularly scan your hard drive to search for malware that may have made it onto your PC. Most AV software runs scheduled scans at regular intervals, but these scans can take a long time (a full scan of my laptop takes more than 90 minutes) and may slow down other applications. You can discontinue a scheduled scan if you find it interfering with your work or play, but be sure to run a full scan as often as possible. Some experts say to scan once a week, but I think only the most hygienically inclined (or paranoid) people actually do that. If you can manage a scan once a month, you should be in good shape.

What AV Software Can't Do

Traditional AV software protection mechanisms cannot protect you from viruses that AV vendors don't know about. As you may have inferred from the paragraph about signatures, the drawback of signature detection is that your AV company has to have a copy of the virus to create a signature. When it comes to brand-new viruses that no one has seen before, AV software won't help. New malware gets a free pass until the AV companies can analyze the malware, create a signature, test it, and distribute it to their customers. Usually this happens within 3 or 4 hours of an outbreak, but if you happen to be unlucky enough to be among the first wave of victims to get infected, you have to wait until your vendor releases a removal utility for the malware. (See the sidebar at the end of this chapter, "Removing a Beagle Worm Variant," for more information.)

Technologies exist that attempt to stop unknown malware by examining the software's behavior for indications that it will do something harmful or unwanted to the computer. For instance, many AV products include a heuristics engine that looks for macro-virus-like characteristics inside code. That same code would be ineffective in detecting a Windows-based Trojan horse or worm. Heuristics engines have proven themselves most effective in finding variants of known malware or polymorphic viruses. Variants are changes made to a known malware program to help evade signature detection, change an attack's payload, or tweak the exploit mechanism used by the malware. Today's worms often include hundreds or thousands of variants that are released on the heels of the original attack. Polymorphic viruses are viruses that are programmed to change their code at regular intervals to try to avoid signature-based scans while still performing the same functions.

However, while heuristics detection can be very effective against certain classes of unknown threats, it doesn't cover all threat types. Another technology, Host Intrusion Prevention Solutions (HIPS), can also stop unknown attacks by examining code for indications of malicious behavior. This technology also stops buffer overflows, a common attack used by malware. A buffer overflow sends more data to an area of the computer's memory (called a buffer) than the computer is expecting. The additional data spills out of the memory buffer and gets executed by the computer. In a buffer overflow exploit, that additional data is usually attack code, which gives the attacker control of the machine. Buffer overflows typically are used by worms, including Code Red, Nimda, and Sasser.

HIPS technology is an important development in security because it is proactive; that is, computers are protected from unknown attacks without having to wait for new signatures to be delivered. Proactive technology is increasingly necessary because new attacks emerge so frequently and spread so rapidly that they can exploit thousands or hundreds of thousands of victims before intrusion or antivirus signatures can be developed.

With that said, the major drawback of HIPS technology is that it's often wrong and attempts to prevent legitimate programs from functioning. When this happens it's called a false positive. False positives have plagued detection technologies for ages and are the main reason that signature-based technology persists—even though it's reactive, it's accurate.

In addition, most HIPS technology is aimed at corporate environments, where the network administrator is better at understanding and defining the security policies that specify how HIPS solutions work. As time goes by it's a safe bet that as these technologies become better understood, more consumer-oriented products will emerge. A number of security products are becoming available, including HIPS technologies such as buffer overflow protection. An example of one such solution is TruPrevent Personal from Panda Software. It's designed as a complement to AV products because its goal is to detect attacks that don't yet have a signature. If you're interested in this technology, Panda Software lets you try TruPrevent before you buy. I recommend that you take advantage of the trial period to see if the software interferes with your computer's normal functions.

4.4 Other Protection Methods

AV software can't always protect you from worms that use infection vectors other than e-mail or instant messaging. AV software may find worms (or the malware that worms deposit on target PCs) during a scan of the hard drive. But to prevent them from hitting your machine in the first place, you need to follow the steps outlined in the rest of this section.

Use a Firewall

As described in Chapter 3, "Firewalls," a firewall can hide your computer from other computers on the Internet. When you have a properly configured firewall in place, worms that are scanning the Internet for vulnerable computers simply skip right over your machine. Consider using security software that bundles multiple features in a single product, including AV software, a firewall, anti-spyware software, and so on. Some firewall and AV software also includes intrusion detection and prevention technology, which looks through incoming Internet traffic for signatures of known worms or other malware. For instance,

Norton AntiVirus includes basic intrusion detection capabilities, while Norton Internet Security includes a full firewall with intrusion detection and prevention. The intrusion detection and prevention software can block any malware for which it has a signature and provides protection for some new operating system vulnerabilities for which there is yet no known exploit or malware code. The intrusion detection and prevention capabilities add another layer of protection against security risks.

Don't Open Strange E-Mail

E-mail is the best thing to happen to computer viruses since the creation of the computer. E-mail provides a communication mechanism to spread viruses, has a list of potential new hosts to infect (all the addresses in your address book), and allows the virus creator to engage in a bit of social engineering to get people to open the message, thus facilitating the virus's spread. That's why you should use caution when reviewing the messages in your inbox. If you see a message from someone you don't know, examine it carefully for the following signs:

- Does the From: address have a strange name, or have an odd structure or strange domain? (The domain is the information on the right of the @ sign.)
- Does the Subject: line contain random characters instead of text? (This indicates that the e-mail was written in a language your e-mail client doesn't support, so it can't properly render the foreign text.) Another warning sign is a blank Subject: line.
- Does the Subject: line contain a sales pitch or an alarmist warning about an account? (Many spammers and phishers are recruiting virus writers to include malware in their junk mail as a kind of bonus. The malware may perform all sorts of functions, from logging your keystrokes to turning your computer into a potential spam bot.)
- Have you received multiple e-mails from the same sender or e-mails that have suspiciously similar subject lines?

If you can answer "Yes" to any of these questions, you should strongly consider deleting the message without opening it. That's because some malware gets activated when you open the e-mail. If you don't want to delete it, don't open it for a day or so. Use that time to check your AV vendor's Web site for alerts about new virus or worm outbreaks. These alerts often include information to help you spot the virus in your own inbox, such as the subject lines used by the virus writer.

Don't Click Links or Programs in E-Mail

If you do open strange mail, don't click any links or programs included in the message. Even if you know the person who sent the e-mail, it may be that he or she was the victim of a virus. Mass-mailing viruses and worms pillage a victim's address book to mail themselves to as many victims as possible, in part because this exploits the trust between correspondents. If you're suspicious of a link sent by someone you know, use another method such as a telephone call to ensure that the sender actually did send the e-mail and that the link or program he or she sent is OK to use. Another option is to retype the link directly into your browser rather than clicking it. This way you know you will not be linked to a malicious site if the link contains hidden characters.

Keep All Your Software Updated

New viruses and worms are created all the time, so you must regularly update your AV software. If your AV software supports automatic updates, you should select this option, because new signatures and other updates are delivered to your computer without your having to do anything. For instance, in Norton AntiVirus, you can turn on Automatic LiveUpdate, a service that sends the latest virus definitions and program updates to your computer whenever you connect to the Internet.

You can also choose whether to have Norton prompt you each time updates are available or have the updates applied to your computer automatically. If you prefer to get new updates on your own, you can also click the Live Update button at the top of the opening screen to download updates manually. Other AV software packages have similar mechanisms for automatic updates.

If automatic updating isn't available on your chosen AV software (and this is unlikely), it should at least have clear instructions on how to access its Web site for new downloads.

You can also protect yourself from malware by keeping other software updated, especially the operating system and applications like Internet Explorer. Chapter 7 provides more details on how to update this software.

4.5 What to Do if You Have a Virus or Worm

Chances are good that even if you keep your defenses up, your computer will get infected someday. But an infection is not cause for panic. You can recover, sometimes quite easily, from a virus or worm attack.

How to Tell if Your Computer Is Infected

The best way to tell if your computer is infected is to run regular AV scans using the latest signature updates. You can also have your computer scanned over the Internet. For instance, the Symantec Security Check scans your computer via the Internet to look for viruses and other malware. To run a free scan, go to www.symantec.com/avcenter/index.html and click the Check for Security Risks icon near the bottom of the page.

You can find similar free services from other AV vendors. At www.mcafee.com, click the Home and Home Office link and look for the Free Tools box on the left side of that opening page. At www.trendmicro.com, click the Personal link. You see the Trend Micro House Call link near the top of the page. This link initiates a free virus scan. Panda Software offers a free scanning tool at http://www.pandasoftware.com/activescan/com/activescan_principal.htm.

However, a scan may not detect a new piece of malware that doesn't yet have a signature. Therefore, keep an eye out for telltale signs that might indicate an infection. For instance, are files damaged or missing, or have settings on an application been changed or security software disabled? Is your computer suddenly sluggish or behaving erratically? Does your firewall detect programs that you haven't opened trying to connect to the Internet? These are all signs that you might have a problem.

How to Remove a Worm or Virus

Once you detect a virus on your computer, you can run your AV software to remove it. Once the scan is complete, the software should prompt you to remove or quarantine any virus it discovered. (To quarantine malware means to leave it on your computer, but in an isolated state where it can't do any harm.) AV software can also clean files that have been infected with a virus.

Your AV vendor will also offer specific tools to remove worms and malware such as Trojan horses (covered in more depth in Chapter 5). You can download these tools from the AV vendor's Web site. Your AV software should be able to recommend whether an additional tool is necessary. In the sidebar "Removing a Beagle Worm Variant" I walk through the steps I took to remove a worm that found its way onto my computer.

In the worst-case scenario the AV software won't be able to remove the malware. If this is the case, you might need outside help. Contact your AV vendor's customer support to see what they recommend (but be prepared for a long wait). You can also contact the computer's manufacturer, seek help from the store where you bought the computer (for a fee, of course), or contact a local computer repair shop for assistance.

As a last resort, you might have to start from scratch and simply reinstall the operating system and applications using the original software discs. To do this, simply insert the original operating system disc into your CD drive and start the computer. The computer prompts you to reconfirm that you want to reinstall the operating system. However, reinstalling the operating system erases all the data you've saved on your computer (let's hope you have good backup habits). Be sure to exhaust all your options before resorting to reformatting your hard drive.

4.6 How to Choose an Anti-Virus Product

If you don't already have an anti-virus product, you have an incredible number of choices. The three largest vendors are Symantec, which sells Norton AntiVirus; Trend Micro, which sells PC-cillin; and McAfee, which sells VirusScan.

The benefits of choosing a solution from one of the big three is that they have well-established research teams that produce new virus signatures in a timely fashion, and they have the infrastructure to distribute these updates to their customer base. The downside is that these solutions tend to be the most expensive.

Close on the heels of the big three are several companies that also offer very good products. They include Computer Associates, Kaspersky Lab, F-Secure, ZoneLabs, ESET, and Panda Software.

You also can get free anti-virus software from an organization called GriSoft. Its AVG Anti-Virus product includes all the common features of paid products. It scans new files and programs and e-mail and lets you run full hard-disk scans. It also offers specialized virus removal tools and includes automatic updates of new virus signatures. The only drawback is that users of the free version don't get any technical support. If you're a registered user, you can post questions to experienced AVG users in an online forum, but you can't e-mail or talk to a support person unless you purchase the paid version. (However, even the paid solution is less expensive than most AV products.)

In general, it's safe to say that all these products provide a similar level of security. Most companies offer a free trial period so that you can sample a variety of programs. Sampling a few programs is a good idea, because it gives you a chance to see which one has the user interface and online documentation you feel most comfortable with. Table 4.3 lists anti-virus vendors, the Web sites where you can get free trials or buy the product. As of mid 2005, prices range from $24.95 to $49.95 for standalone anti-virus software, though special offers and rebates may affect the final cost. As mentioned earlier, you will get better value from a product that includes other security functions in addition to virus protection.

Table 4.3

Leading Anti-Virus Products

Product	Vendor	Web Site
Anti-Virus Personal	Kaspersky Lab	www.kaspersky.com
AVG Anti-Virus	GriSoft	http://free.grisoft.com
eTrust Antivirus	Computer Associates	www.ca.com
F-Secure Anti-Virus	F-Secure	www.f-secure.com
NOD32	ESET	www.eset.com
Norton AntiVirus	Symantec	www.symantec.com
PC-cillin	Trend Micro	www.trendmicro.com
Titanium Antivirus	Panda Software	www.pandasoftware.com
VirusScan	McAfee	www.mcafee.com
ZoneAlarm AntiVirus	Zone Labs	www.zonelabs.com

If you're looking for more advice, magazines and Web sites such as *PC Magazine* (www.pcmagazine.com), *PC World* (www.pcworld.com), and CNET (www.cnet.com) regularly review consumer security products and usually pick an "editor's choice." You can read reviews and compare prices and features on these Web sites.

4.7 Checklist

Use this checklist as a quick-reference guide to the material covered in this chapter.

Do

- Use anti-virus software, whether standalone or as part of a bundled solution.
- Perform regular scans of your computer, and keep your anti-virus software updated.
- Keep your operating system and browser software updated.
- Perform regular backups of essential files.

Don't

- Open suspicious or unsolicited e-mail from people you don't know.
- Click links inside e-mail or open attachments from strangers.

4.8 Helpful Resources

This section presents additional resources to help you learn more.

All the AV vendors listed in this chapter include information about virus outbreaks, the latest AV updates, and removal tools. They also include tips on avoiding malware infection and securing your PC.

Virus List, at www.viruslist.com, run by AV vendor Kaspersky Lab, is an excellent resource for information about malware, spam, malicious attackers, and general Internet security issues. The site includes an encyclopedia of malware topics and tips to help make your computer more secure.

The Virus Bulletin, at www.virusbtn.com, includes a host of information about viruses and malware. It also sells a newsletter with information from the anti-virus research community.

The WildList Organization, at www.wildlist.org, considers itself to be a reality check for anti-virus vendors, which may inflate claims about the number of viruses in existence. There's some merit to this. Depending on which vendor's numbers you use, the virus population is anywhere from 50,000 to 90,000 and rising. However, the number of viruses that have spread significantly is considerably smaller.

This organization tracks viruses that are considered to be affecting normal computer users during day-to-day operations. Viruses "in the wild" are contrasted with viruses that are discovered in the laboratory by researchers or that are released as proofs of concept without actually spreading. The WildList relies on volunteers from the anti-virus research community and others to contribute virus samples and track viruses in the wild.

Removing a Beagle Worm Variant

In late January 2005, my home computer was infected with a variant of the Beagle worm called Beagle.BA. (Most AV products call this the Bagle worm.) A variant is a new version of a previously released piece of malware. Variants occur when malware writers take an existing virus or worm and make changes and additions to the software. Beagle.BA was a mass-mailing worm that also attempted to shut down anti-virus and security software running on the host machine. This is not an uncommon technique for worms, especially those that attempt to insert a Trojan horse on the computer so that the machine can be used by an attacker later. Luckily for me, Beagle.BA didn't carry a Trojan horse in its payload.

I discovered I was infected when a regular hard-drive scan uncovered the worm. Norton AntiVirus deleted the worm from my computer, but it also recommended that I download a special repair tool to fix any damage the worm might have caused when installing itself on my computer.

I surfed to www.symantec.com and clicked the Security Response link, which brought me to the Security Response home page. At that time the Beagle.BA variant was still listed on the first page of Security Response, so I clicked the link, which took me directly to the Beagle.BA removal tool. (If you can't find a particular virus listed on the first page of Security Response, you can enter the name into a search field to find the right page.)

continues . . .

The instructions on the Web page recommended that I turn off System Restore. System Restore is a function in Windows that monitors changes to the essential system files and registries that allow the operating system to function. You can use System Restore to create a snapshot of a known, good state when your computer is operating properly. If something disrupts proper operations, you can use System Restore to revert to that known good state.

However, malware often saves itself in system files and registries, so it's possible that System Restore might save a worm or virus and reinstall the malware on your computer. By disabling System Restore, you remove all the previous restore points stored there. To learn more about System Restore, click Start, click the Help and Support button, and type **System Restore overview** into the search field.

Temporarily disabling System Restore does not affect your personal files, such as Word documents, images, and media. To disable System Restore, click Start, and then select Control Panel. (Depending on how you've set up your Start menu, you may have to click Settings to find the Control Panel option.) When you click Control Panel, a window opens that says Pick a category, as shown in Figure 4.1.

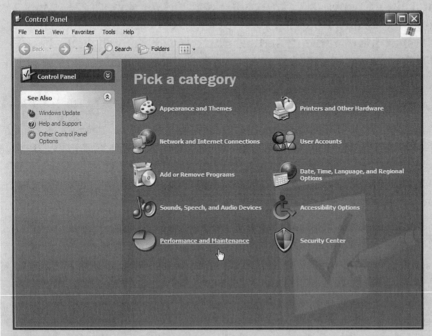

Figure 4.1   The Performance and Maintenance category in Control Panel.

Choose the Performance and Maintenance category, and then click the System option, as shown in Figure 4.2. A smaller window titled System Properties appears, as shown in Figure 4.3. This window has multiple tabs, such as General, Computer Name, and Hardware. Select the System Restore tab. You see a checkbox labeled Turn off System Restore. Check the box and click the Apply button at the bottom of the window.

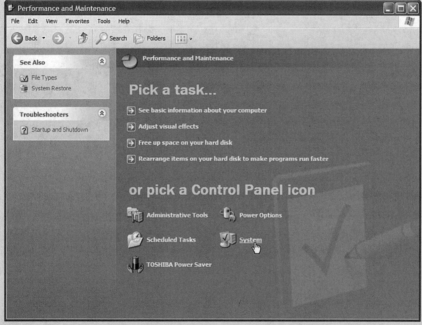

Figure 4.2   The System category in Performance and Maintenance.

After I did this, I downloaded the tool, called FxBeagle, and ran it on my computer. When the tool finished, I made my way back to the System Restore window and turned System Restore back on. Afterward I did a full disk scan one more time to ensure that my computer was clean.

continues . . .

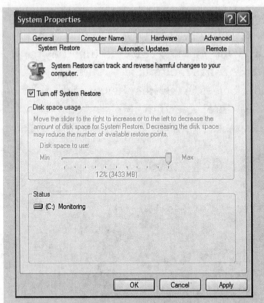

Figure 4.3   The System Properties dialog box.

If you are confident that your computer is clean, you can also set your own restore point. To set a restore point, click Start, and then choose All Programs, Accessories, System Tools, and System Restore. A wizard walks you through the steps necessary to set restore points.

Chapter 5

Getting Rid of Unwanted Guests, Part 2: Spyware, Adware, and Trojan Horses

The preceding chapter discussed the rise of malware and examined two particular species of malware: viruses and worms. This chapter examines three other distinct kinds of security risks: spyware, adware, and Trojan horses. We'll spend some time defining each of these risks, look at the legal and technological challenges of dealing with spyware and adware, and discuss how to protect yourself from these threats.

5.1 What Are Spyware, Adware, and Trojan Horses?

In a narrow sense, spyware is a term for some tracking technologies (specifically, executable applications) deployed on your computer without adequate notice, consent, or control. Spyware can monitor your activities online and/or perform functions without your knowledge or consent. Depending on the program, spyware can track and report on every Web site you visit, generate pop-up advertising, change your home page and browser settings, or record every key you press. In its broader sense, spyware is also commonly used as the overall name for most types of potentially unwanted technologies detected by popular anti-spyware programs. These technologies are implemented in ways that impair your control over the following: collection, use, and distribution of your personal information; material changes that affect your desktop experience, privacy, or system security; and use of your system resources. These are items that users of anti-spyware software will want to be informed about and that they may want to easily remove or disable.

Adware is a subset of the broader spyware category, which is designed to deliver targeted advertising to your Web browser, especially through the use of pop-up ads. Adware is often bundled with other software programs, such as peer-to-peer file-sharing software, games, or other utilities that can be downloaded for free from the Web. Adware knows what kinds of ads to deliver to you because it tracks the places you surf. For instance, if you surf to a car rental site, an adware program might generate a pop-up ad that a competing car rental company has paid the adware company to deliver to you. Besides tracking your behavior and annoying you with ads, adware may also open a connection on the Internet to report your surfing habits back to a central server. This information, which may include your age, your sex, your shopping habits, and even your location, is used to conduct "market research" to attract new clients.

Trojan horses are programs that claim to be something they are not. For instance, a Trojan horse may advertise itself as an amusing animation clip, a screen saver, or a free software program that promises to do something cool or helpful. But Trojan horses also include unadvertised functions (if, in fact, the advertised function works at all). The most common goal of a Trojan horse is to install a back door on your computer or steal passwords. A back door lets attackers control your machine remotely. Some classes of spyware can be considered Trojan horses because they arrive under false pretenses. For instance, you may have downloaded a neat little screen saver with pretty butterflies on it that also happens to monitor your Web-surfing habits or log your keystrokes. Trojan horses often rely on viruses, worms, and social engineering to get unsuspecting users to download them.

The term Trojan horse has become shorthand for any program that resides on your computer and provides remote access to an unauthorized person or performs unwanted functions. Most anti-virus (AV) software and some anti-spyware software can detect Trojan horses.

Spyware, adware, and Trojan horses can't replicate themselves. Thus, these categories of applications need other ways to spread. For instance, Trojan horses may be delivered as part of the payload of a worm or virus, included as an e-mail attachment, or bundled with other software. Spyware and adware use similar techniques to spread, but they are most frequently downloaded as part of a "free" file-sharing program or software utility or via drive-by downloads (in which you visit a Web site that installs the program without your permission).

Defining Spyware and Adware

While security risks such as spyware and adware can be seen as an extension of the virus problem, there are significant differences in how these programs are judged as desirable or undesirable and whether you want them on your machine. Viruses, worms, and Trojan horses are always undesirable and should be automatically removed from a computer. Many types of programs classified as adware and spyware are also high-risk and can have a significant negative impact on computer performance or invade your privacy by transmitting personal information to a third party.

However, other adware programs are low-risk. They can deliver useful functionality such as games or utilities and have a relatively small impact on privacy and computer performance. Just as broadcast television programs are free because television companies earn revenue from advertising, many software programs are free to download because they too rely on advertising to generate income. Such software programs are called ad-supported programs. They include adware to deliver targeted ads. Some ad-supported software programs seek the user's consent before installing adware; others do not. Still others operate in a gray area in which user consent is part of the "fine print" of a software license agreement. We'll examine these distinctions and what they mean to you more closely in subsequent sections.

The broad range of spyware and adware or potentially unwanted programs can be divided into two general categories: high-risk or malicious programs and low-risk programs. Security researchers assign spyware and adware programs to one of these categories depending on how the programs are installed, what data they try to export from your computer, what impact they have on your computer's performance, and what you are led to understand about their operation and intent. When security researchers investigate a program's behaviors to determine risk, they look at a number of key areas, including installation characteristics, stealth properties, privacy impact, integrity impact, performance impact, and ease of removal:

- Does the program impact system stability or slow down the network connection?
- Does the program launch pop-up advertisements? If so, how frequently?
- Does the program serve as a means of downloading and installing other security risks (such as additional spyware and/or adware)?

- Does the program replace the browser home page or alter search options or behavior?
- Does the program cause the release of confidential, sensitive information such as bank account numbers and passwords?
- Does the program cause the release of less-sensitive data such as tracking of Web-surfing habits?
- Does the program have a privacy policy, and does its behavior match the stated policy?
- Does the program try to hide itself or avoid being uninstalled by the user, including an unsolicited reinstallation and techniques to restart user-terminated processes?
- Does the program lack an uninstall feature or fail to register in the Microsoft Windows Add or Remove Programs area?
- Does the program install itself silently, with little or no indication to the user?
- Does the program lack a user interface?
- Does the program conceal its processes or hide them from the user using an obscure name?
- Is the user notified of the program's presence only through an End User License Agreement (EULA)? Does the EULA appear to relate to a different program?

To qualify as high-risk or malicious spyware and adware, programs must have significant impact on system stability and/or performance or release confidential, sensitive information and/or exhibit stealth behaviors such as a silent installation, no user interface, and concealment of application processes. Examples of high-risk programs can include keystroke loggers, browser hijackers, and dialers. (Table 5.1 describes these and other kinds of programs.) Malicious spyware is illegal and therefore is employed by criminals who want to steal from you. Malicious spyware gets installed on your computer through software vulnerabilities, worms and viruses, social engineering, and drive-by downloads.

Low-risk programs include many popular commercial adware or ad-assisted programs. However, some adware generates multiple pop-up ads and performs other unwanted functions, like changing your home page, directing you to unfamiliar search engines, or installing toolbars in your Web browser that you didn't

Table 5.1

Spyware Definitions	
Term	**Definition**
Spyware	Spyware is a general class of software programs that monitor computer activity and relay that information to other computers or locations on the Internet. Among the information that may be actively or passively gathered and transmitted by spyware are passwords, log-in details, account numbers, personal information, individual files, and personal documents. Spyware may also gather and distribute information related to the user's computer, applications running on the computer, Internet browser usage, and other computing habits. Spyware is usually loaded onto a user's computer without the user's knowledge and is created by underground attackers or criminals.
Adware	Adware is a type of advertising display technology—specifically, executable applications whose primary purpose is to deliver advertising content. Many adware applications also perform tracking functions and therefore may also be categorized as tracking technologies. Consumers may want to remove adware if they object to such tracking, do not want to see the advertising generated by the program, or are frustrated by its effects on system performance. Some users might want to keep particular adware programs if their presence is a condition for the use of other free software. Adware is created by commercial software companies rather than criminals and is often bundled with popular free software, such as file-sharing programs. Some adware describes its functions in a license agreement and provides uninstall options; other adware may install itself without a user's permission and thwart attempts at removal.
Keystroke logger (also known as a keylogger)	Keyloggers are tracking technologies that surreptitiously record keyboard activity. Keyloggers typically either store the recorded keystrokes for later retrieval or transmit them to the remote process or person employing the keylogger via e-mail. Keystroke loggers are used to steal passwords and other identity information.
Browser hijacker	Browser hijackers reset your home page and redirect your browser to unwanted or unknown search engines or other Web sites. Some browser hijackers can prevent you from restoring your home page. Browser hijackers work by deleting the entry for the home page you've selected and inserting their own in a special file that your computer consults (the hosts file). They also might intercept search queries typed into a legitimate search engine and display their own results.

Term	Definition
Browser Helper Object (BHO)	BHOs are companion applications for Microsoft Internet Explorer (IE) that run automatically whenever IE is launched. They are a form of state management tool. Many tracking technologies or advertising display technologies are implemented as BHOs. BHOs can search the Web pages a user visits and replace banner ads generated by the Web server with targeted ads. BHOs can also monitor and report on a user's surfing behavior and may reset a user's home page. Note that not all BHOs are malicious; many legitimate Web browser toolbars are BHOs.
Trojan horse	Trojan horse software masquerades as an innocuous or useful program to trick a user into installing it. Once installed, the Trojan horse engages in unwanted or unadvertised functions.
Remote Access/ Administration Tool (RAT)	RATs are executable applications designed to allow remote access to or control of a system. They are a type of remote-control technology. Many legitimate uses of RATs do not pose security threats, but they can be used maliciously, especially when used by someone other than the computer's legitimate owner or administrator.
Dialer	Dialers are programs that use a computer's modem to make calls or access services. Users may want to remove dialers that can result in unexpected phone numbers being dialed or unexpected telephone charges. Dialer is a colloquial term for dialing technologies.

seek out and don't want. Adware may also read cookies installed on your computer to find out information about you and your Web habits.

Of course, regardless of whether a program is high- or low-risk, you, the user, should have absolute control over the programs on your computer, including the ability to find and remove any programs you don't want. As you'll see in the following section, some spyware and adware attempts to usurp that control.

5.2 Technical and Legal Challenges of Detecting and Removing Spyware and Adware

Chapter 4, "Getting Rid of Unwanted Guests, Part 1: Viruses and Worms," talked about several reasons for the rise of malware (ease of communication, a homogenous computing environment, reactive security software). Those factors certainly apply to the rise of spyware, but the undeniable *raison d'être* of spyware and adware is money. Whether facilitating identity theft, recruiting your computer into a rentable bot network, or generating advertising revenue for shady software companies, this type of application is increasingly influenced by dollar signs. The potential profits that can be generated make the spyware/adware problem inherently more difficult to solve. Spyware brokers can hire programmers to continually tweak the code to better avoid detection and removal by security software or encourage the development of open-source or professional library programs.

Just how profitable a business is it? Consider this: An adware company called Claria earned approximately $90 million in 2003. (Claria's adware products are known as GAIN or Gator, and they often come bundled with third-party software such as Kazaa, the peer-to-peer software.) With profits like this, adware companies have strong motivation to continue what they are doing. Other adware companies include WhenU., 180Solutions, Avenue Media, and Direct Revenue.

Numerous indicators demonstrate the pervasiveness of spyware and adware. The Internet service provider (ISP) Earthlink conducted a study with WebRoot, which makes anti-spyware software. They scanned more than 3.2 million PCs and found an average of 26 spyware programs per PC. Dell Computer says spyware problems are the number one cause of tech support calls. Symantec conducted a study to see which categories of Web sites left behind the most unwanted software. Researchers took a brand-new Windows PC out of the box, connected it to the Internet without any standard protection software, and browsed. Testers spent one hour each interacting with different categories of Web sites. Surprisingly, children's Web sites dumped the most unwanted software on a PC—359 pieces of adware in just an hour's surfing. By comparison, the second-highest total was 64 pieces of adware installed from travel sites. Gaming sites dumped the most spyware—four pieces. Table 5.2 lists the full results.

Table 5.2

Symantec's "Unwanted Software" Study				
Site Category	**Adware**	**Spyware**	**Hijackers**	**Cookies**
Gaming	23	4	2	68
Kids	359	0	3	31
News	3	1	0	26
Reseller	2	1	1	22
Shopping	0	0	0	10
Sports	17	2	0	72
Travel	64	2	1	35

Creators of high-risk adware and spyware tend to make their software difficult to find and get rid of. For instance, a spyware program may put thousands of files on a PC and make thousands of changes to the Registry. The Registry is a database of configuration settings that tells the computer about the applications and user profiles on your machine. Your computer refers to the Registry at startup and each time you open programs. Spyware and adware often insert themselves into the Registry to become one of the programs that the computer runs automatically.

Spyware and adware may put two copies of themselves on your PC so that if you delete one, the backup copy will still run. Or they may plant "tricklers" on your computer. Tricklers are tiny pieces of software that download unwanted programs a little bit at a time each time the computer is connected to the Internet, until the entire program is installed.

Legitimate software is relatively easy to uninstall using the Add or Remove Programs function in Windows XP, shown in Figure 5.1. It basically lists all the programs on your computer and gives you the option to uninstall each one individually. One of the indicators of a high-risk adware or spyware program is that it doesn't appear in the list of programs. To see the list of programs on your PC, click the Start button and then choose Add/Remove. If Add/Remove is not on your Start menu, choose Control Panel and then Add or Remove Programs. A legitimate adware program would appear in this area and allow you to remove it.

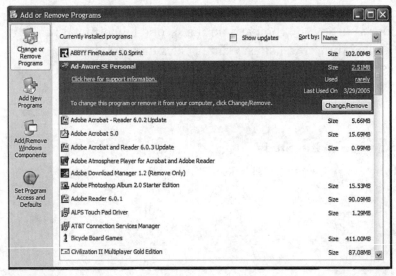

Figure 5.1   Add or Remove Programs.

Some spyware even goes so far as installing itself without your permission (for instance, even if you click "No, I don't want this program," it still installs itself) or without your knowledge (a drive-by download). All of these characteristics make spyware and adware difficult to find and remove.

Some adware companies claim they are trying to become better Internet citizens. For instance, Claria and WhenU. say they have sworn off dirty tricks like drive-by downloads to install their software on consumers' PCs. (But some researchers argue they still make it difficult for users to find and uninstall their programs.)

Other adware vendors don't even bother with appearances of legitimacy and continue to play dirty, even with each other. For instance, in 2004, Avenue Media accused DirectRevenue of creating software to find and remove Avenue Media's adware and install its own on consumer PCs.

Besides the technical challenges of preventing and removing spyware and adware, there are also legal issues to deal with. While some categories of spyware are overtly against the law (such as keystroke loggers), adware enjoys a quasi-legal status. For instance, any adware that notifies users of its functions in a EULA is, for the most part, legal. That's because you, the user, are supposed to read and agree to the conditions contained in the EULA. Before the download commences, you must click a button that says something like "I agree to the terms and conditions set forth in this license." Clicking such a button is akin to signing a physical contract; once you click yes, you agree to whatever the EULA says. However, almost no one bothers to read EULAs, and the adware companies know it. (See the sidebar at the end of this chapter, "Reading the Fine Print," for more information.)

Its advisable to seek out and read the EULA for any sites you visit or programs you download. If a program has no EULA or tries to hide its intent behind confusing language, take this as a warning sign, and strongly consider not downloading the program.

However, one of the issues under debate regarding adware EULAs is figuring out what constitutes sufficient notice and consent. If an adware program actually describes its functions in a EULA, does that count as sufficient notice? What if that description is buried inside a long agreement and is vaguely or confusingly worded?

A number of federal legislative solutions have been proposed recently to address spyware and adware, including the issue of sufficient notice and consent. As of June 1, 2005, two bills had been introduced in the House and two in the Senate. In the House of Representatives, legislation known as the SPY ACT (Securely Protect Yourself Against Computer Trespassers, H.R. 29), is sponsored by Congresswoman Mary Bono. The SPY ACT would generally make unacceptable behavior, such as installing software without your permission, illegal. The bill also stipulates that adware vendors must clearly state the software's functions, the types of information being collected, and the purposes for collecting the information. The bill also says adware must give consumers the ability to decline installation or remove the software at any time without "undue effort." Another House bill, the I-SPY Prevention Act of 2005 (H.R. 744), was introduced by Congressman Bob Goodlatte on February 10, 2005. It focuses largely on taking enforcement action and stiffening penalties against the bad guys. This bill adds a new Section 1030A to the Criminal Code titled "Illicit indirect use of protected computers" and creates three criminal prohibitions.

In the Senate, the SPY BLOCK Act (S. 687) was introduced by Senator Conrad Burns with Senators Ron Wyden and Barbara Boxer on March 20, 2005. The Act would prohibit installing software on somebody else's computer without notice and consent and requires reasonable uninstall procedures for all downloadable software. The Enhanced Consumer Protection Against Spyware Act of 2005, introduced by Senator Allen with Senators Smith and Ensign on May 11, 2005, would allow for the seizing of profits from companies and individuals secretly installing spyware on computers. It would seek significantly higher civil and criminal penalties for those trafficking in spyware. It also would beef up the Federal Trade Commission's authority to prosecute spyware intrusions.

All four of the bills recognize that many of the technologies used for malicious and deceptive practices can also be used for beneficial and legitimate purposes. According to the legislation, being adware or spyware doesn't necessarily make the technology bad or illegal. The bills only seek to regulate the misuse of adware and spyware.

As of June 1, 2005, H.R. 29 and H.R. 744 had both been passed in the House. What remains is for the Senate to vote on its own two bills, and then for the House and Senate to agree on a combined bill that would pass both houses. Finally, the president would have to sign the bill into law.

You can read all four bills by going to Thomas, a search page run by the Library of Congress for finding legislation online. Go to http://thomas.loc.gov and type the bill's name or number into the search field for the 109th Congress.

In addition to the federal legislative activity this year, more than 40 spyware bills have been introduced in state legislatures.

The Federal Trade Commission has also taken notice of the spyware problem. In March 2005, the commission released a report titled "Monitoring Software on Your PC: Spyware, Adware, and Other Software." The report outlines the problems associated with defining spyware, the risks spyware presents to consumers, and how government and industry leaders can respond to the spyware problem. To find a copy of the report, see the "Helpful Resources" section near the end of this chapter.

Legal issues have also complicated the efforts of anti-spyware vendors to deal with adware. In 2003, Claria sued PC PitStop, an anti-spyware organization, for defamation. PC PitStop was calling Claria's products spyware, and the company didn't appreciate it. In 2005, the makers of the popular WeatherBug software complained when Microsoft's anti-spyware product listed an ad-serving component inside WeatherBug as a privacy risk. Microsoft reviewed the complaint and removed the signature that detected the ad server.

Some anti-spyware products have found themselves at cross-purposes with other business units inside the same company. The online portal Yahoo! offers a free anti-spyware program in its Yahoo! toolbar. But when the product was first launched, it required users to specifically request a scan for adware in addition to spyware. That's because Yahoo!'s Overture division, which provides paid search listings, is a business partner of Claria Corporation. According to a June 2004 story in *eWeek*,[1] Overture provided paid listings to SearchScout, a Claria service that displays "pop-under" advertising. (These ads show up under the page; you see them after you close the browser.) SearchScout was responsible for 31 percent of Claria's revenue in 2003. Yahoo! has since changed its anti-spyware toolbar to search for adware in addition to spyware.

One way for anti-spyware companies to avoid trouble is by adopting more diplomatic language. For instance, McAfee's anti-spyware software uses the term

---

1. *"Yahoo Plays Favorites with Some Adware," by Matt Hicks, published on June 1, 2004 in eWeek (www.eweek.com).*

"Potentially Unwanted Programs" rather than "adware" or "spyware." Microsoft's anti-spyware software also skirts the issue by referring to everything as "Potentially Unwanted Software." (If you turn that into an acronym, it spells PUS. I don't know if the folks at Microsoft chose it on purpose, but it generally sums up the feelings of people who have to deal with this kind of thing. It's also shorter than my own term, which also can be turned into an acronym: Bad, Annoying Software That All of us Require be Deleted Speedily.)

Do You Want a Cookie?

Cookies present another difficulty with classifying and dealing with intrusive or unwanted programs. Cookies are small text files that a Web server places on your computer when you visit a Web site. Cookies contain information about you such as your user preferences or log-in information. Each time you return to a Web site, the appropriate cookie is transmitted from your computer to the Web site to help customize your visit. For instance, if you're a regular customer of an e-commerce site, that site might store information about you in a cookie on your PC, such as your shopping history, purchase preferences, and so on. Cookies facilitate the e-commerce experience and generally are benign.

However, another category of cookie, called a tracking cookie, records information about other Web sites you visit and shares that information with other sites. Advertising networks collect this information to conduct market research and help them serve targeted ads on your computer. Good anti-spyware software should detect tracking cookies and give you the option of deleting them.

You can see the cookies on your computer by going to My Computer. Click the Local Disk (C:) folder, then Documents and Settings, then your username, and then the Cookies folder. However, looking at cookies won't tell you much about whether it's a standard cookie or a tracking cookie. Most cookies consist of lots of numbers that have meaning to a Web server, but not a human. However, by looking at the Cookies list you can see which Web sites are setting cookies on your hard drive. You can delete them by highlighting the specific file and clicking the Delete this file command on the left side of the window, as shown in Figure 5.2.

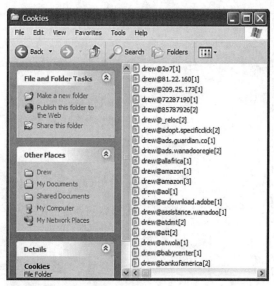

Figure 5.2   Deleting cookies.

You also can control how and whether Web sites can set cookies on your computer by adjusting your privacy settings in your Web browser. If you're using Internet Explorer, open the browser and select Tools, Internet Options, Privacy. A slider bar adjusts the privacy setting and tells the Web browser what kinds of cookies it accepts, as shown in Figure 5.3. Options range from accepting all cookies to blocking all cookies, with various gradations in between. Microsoft's default setting is Medium High, which means your browser blocks any cookies that attempt to use personally identifiable information without your explicit consent.

Remember, not all cookies are invasive. For instance, if you delete cookies from e-commerce sites you use regularly, you may find that the customization you enjoyed has been wiped out. Also, setting your cookie protection too high might lock you out of sites. For instance, my Yahoo! Web mail account wouldn't work with the Block All Cookies or High security settings in Internet Explorer. Cookie setting is discussed in more depth in Chapter 7, "Securing Windows."

Figure 5.3   Setting cookie options in IE.

Another example of such tracking objects are Local Shared Objects (LSOs), which are best thought of as Macromedia Flash program cookies. A Web site can use an LSO to store information on your computer such as a game's high score or information you have filled in (such as your name and age). Unlike with a cookie, however, you cannot disable LSOs through your normal browser settings.

5.3 How Spyware/Adware and Trojan Horses Infect Your Computer

Spyware, adware, and Trojan horses can get onto your machine in a number of ways, including from a Web browser, via e-mail, or in a bundle with other software you download. By knowing how this software gets on your machine, you'll have a better idea of how to keep it out.

From a Web Browser

One of the reasons that Web browsing is a popular spyware/adware vehicle is ActiveX. ActiveX is a Microsoft technology that is designed to enable easier embedding of interactive objects, and often multimedia, on Web pages. ActiveX helps make Web pages more interactive, such as through animation or through the ability to open other applications in a browser (such as Microsoft Word or Adobe).

Besides enlivening Web pages, ActiveX technology can also execute programs, called ActiveX controls, on your computer via the Internet Explorer Web browser. ActiveX controls interact with the operating system just like any other executable software. ActiveX programs come with digital signatures from the program's author (that is, the company that created the program, not the actual software engineer). Think of a digital signature as being like a person's signature on paper. Your browser can look at a digital signature and see whether it is genuine so that you can know for sure who signed a program. You have two choices: either accept the program and let it do whatever it wants on your machine, or reject it. ActiveX security relies on you to make correct decisions about which programs to accept. Some ActiveX controls are harmless and improve your browsing experience, but malware writers can also create ActiveX controls to install unwanted programs on your computer. If you accept a malicious program, you're in big trouble.

You can adjust your Internet Explorer browser to prompt you when an ActiveX control wants to download to your computer. To find out how, see the section "Adjust Your Browser Settings."

Spyware and malware writers can also exploit software vulnerabilities in browsers (including alternative browsers such as Mozilla Firefox). Every software product in the world has defects that are discovered by researchers. Some of these researchers are security professionals; others are malicious attackers who use the discovery to attack the vulnerable software. Because Internet Explorer is the world's most widely used browser, it's a popular target for attackers. For instance, in June 2004 a Trojan horse called Download.ject emerged. Using a vulnerability in IE and IIS (Internet Information Server, which is Windows' Web server software), the Trojan horse installed itself on people's computers if they simply visited a Web site running on an infected Web server. Download.ject is an example of a drive-by download. Attacks that exploit software vulnerabilities are best dealt with by applying software fixes called patches, which are created and distributed by the software vendor. For instance, on the second Tuesday of every month, Microsoft releases the latest round of patches for its software. To download patches, go to http://windowsupdate.microsoft.com.

From Other Software

The most common method of spreading adware is to include it with other programs, such as file-sharing software or fun, cutesy utilities. Sometimes the provider of the software you want tells you that adware is also being installed. Sometimes it doesn't. In many cases, the software you want, such as a file-sharing program, doesn't work if you disable the adware that comes with it. (See the later sidebar "Reading the Fine Print.")

From E-Mail

Spyware and Trojan horses may get onto your computer as e-mail attachments. For instance, many phishing attacks, in which a scam artist uses e-mail to trick you into revealing passwords, Social Security numbers, and other sensitive information, also includes malware such as keystroke loggers.

From Social Engineering

As discussed in Chapter 2, "Preventing Identity Theft," social engineering is a fancy way to describe a lie. Spyware and adware purveyors aren't above lying to get you to install software. The most common example of social engineering is to advertise a program or e-mail attachment as something that it isn't. A great example is the Naked Wife worm that showed up in 2001. It spread by e-mail and included an attachment that purported to be a naughty Flash movie. In fact, the attachment was a Trojan horse that would install itself on your computer, mail itself to everyone in your e-mail address book, and then start deleting files.

5.4 How to Protect Yourself from Spyware, Adware, and Trojan Horses

You can protect your computer from becoming infected with spyware, adware, and Trojan horses in a variety of ways. This section outlines several methods.

Use Anti-Spyware and Anti-Virus Software

The best way to protect yourself from spyware and Trojan horses is to use anti-spyware and anti-virus software. Both kinds of software can prevent known spyware and Trojan horses from being installed on your computer, and they may be able to prevent unknown malware as well.

Many anti-virus vendors now offer spyware and adware protection as part of a larger product suite that includes anti-virus software and a firewall. These suites are a great option because they are easier to manage than a handful of disparate stand-alone products. Also, you don't have to worry about Product A causing Product B to malfunction (or Products A and B together causing your computer to malfunction).

That said, you still may want additional protection from dedicated anti-spyware software. Why? The simplest reason is the defense-in-depth strategy (also known as the belt-and-suspenders approach); one product might catch spyware or adware that the other product misses.

So why not have two different anti-virus products as well? In fact, many corporations employ this very strategy: E-mail servers get loaded with anti-virus software from AV company number 1, while corporate desktops get anti-virus software from AV company number 2. However, consumers don't really need two different anti-virus products because, generally speaking, the AV vendors have established parity—each AV provider does about as good a job as the others.

That's not necessarily the case when it comes to spyware and adware. Security software companies are still struggling to define exactly what spyware and adware are. Each company has its own set of definitions, which means that each company identifies and deals with spyware and adware in slightly different ways. On top of that, spyware and adware writers have proven to be clever and innovative, and they are constantly finding new ways to burrow into your computer. New spyware and adware emerges at an incredible rate, and one company may have signatures before another company does, or one company may deploy a removal tool faster than another. The result is that Company A's anti-spyware protection may excel in some areas but stink in others, and vice versa for Company B.

You can purchase stand-alone anti-spyware software from a number of vendors, and you also have several good free options. So even if your AV software already scans for spyware, you might want to double-check it with another anti-spyware tool. Tables 5.3 and 5.4 list leading anti-spyware software, both paid and free versions.

That said, if you do run two separate anti-spyware programs, don't be surprised if they start causing problems. If that's the case, you have to decide which one you like better and abandon the other.

Top names in the anti-spyware market include Aluria Software which makes Spyware Eliminator; Sunbelt Software, which makes CounterSpy; Webroot Software, which makes Spy Sweeper; Lavasoft, which makes Ad-Aware; Tenebril, which makes SpyCatcher; and Computer Associates, which sells eTrust PestPatrol. Established anti-virus vendors also sell anti-spyware tools, and smaller vendors also offer decent products. Table 5.3 lists vendors. As of mid-2005, pricing ranges from $19.95 to $29.95 for standalone anti-spyware software, and $49.95 to $69.95 for security suites that include anti-spyware, anti-virus, a firewall, and

Table 5.3

Commercial Anti-Spyware Products		
Product	**Vendor**	**Web Site**
ActiveScan Pro	Panda Software	www.pandasoftware.com
Ad-Aware SE Plus	Lavasoft	www.lavasoft.com
CounterSpy	Sunbelt Software	www.sunbeltsoftware.com
eTrust PestPatrol	Computer Associates	www.ca.com
F-Secure Anti-Spyware for Windows	F-Secure	www.f-secure.com
McAfee Antispyware	McAfee	www.mcafee.com
PC-cillin	Trend Micro	www.trendmicro.com
SpyCatcher	Tenebril	www.tenebril.com
Spy Sweeper	Webroot Software	www.webroot.com
Spyware Eliminator	Aluria Software	www.aluriasoftware.com
Symantec Norton Internet Security Spyware Edition	Symantec	www.symantec.com

other security products. Note that special offers and rebates may affect the final cost.

When choosing a product, look for a system that lets you conduct regular scans and perform real-time detection of potential spyware. Look for products that can detect and remove spyware and quarantine suspicious programs. (A quarantine function keeps the program from operating but does not remove it. Quarantining allows you to investigate whether a program should be removed.)

Like firewalls and AV products, anti-spyware products ask you to decide what to do with the programs they detect. Sometimes the decision is easy, but other times you may not be sure. Anti-spyware programs often provide information about the programs detected, but that information may be so technical that it doesn't help. Therefore, look for a product that includes significant information presented intelligibly to help you make that decision.

You also have to keep the software updated. Look for an interface that makes updates easy—or, better still, that automates the update process. Take advantage of free trials to test and see which interface you find the most useful.

To help you decide which product to choose, check out reviews from *PC Magazine* (www.pcmagazine.com), *PC World* (www.pcworld.com), and CNET (www.cnet.com), which regularly review and rate security products. You can also check online forums for recommendations and reviews. Good forums are available at CastleCops (www.castlecops.com) and SpywareInfo (www.spywareinfo.com).

Beware of Opportunists

Anti-virus products have been around for years. In that time inferior or shady products have gone away, while at the same time a reputable group of companies have developed stable products that generally work as advertised. The anti-spyware market is in its infancy, and market forces that trim weak or disreputable businesses have yet to exert their full influence. Many products are rushed onto the market, and they just don't work very well. Some products also try to confuse users by taking names or registering Web sites that are similar to popular anti-spyware software. For instance, the name of a popular anti-browser-hijacking tool called HijackThis is often used by imitators or malware purveyors hoping to attract unsuspecting users to their own sites. The real HijackThis tool is available at www.merijn.org/downloads.html.

In addition, the opportunities presented by a hot new technology sector also attract those who aren't above unsavory (and illegal) tactics to convince you to buy their software. For instance, in March 2005 the FTC filed a complaint against a product called Spyware Assassin. According to the FTC, Spyware Assassin offered deceptive free scans that claimed to detect spyware on users' computers, even when no spyware was present. The scam even went as far as listing names and file locations of spyware on computers that were clean. Spyware Assassin then offered anti-spyware software (at $29.95 a pop), which the FTC says doesn't even work that well.

If you haven't specifically visited a site to request a scan, be suspicious of unsolicited and alarmist pop-ups that urge you to click or scan immediately—or that claim to have detected spyware on your computer without your having even requested a scan. As you would in the real world, be wary of such high-pressure sales tactics.

The vendors listed in this chapter are reputable, and you should feel comfortable doing business with them. If a vendor isn't listed here, that doesn't imply that its product is defective or misleading. That said, if you're dealing with a new or little-known company, be cautious. For instance, reputable companies always have a clearly posted EULA and privacy policy on their Web site. One way to check out a company is to search for the name and see what results come back. You can also post to an anti-spyware forum to get a sense of a company's reputation or to find out if others have had positive or negative experiences.

Free Anti-Spyware Software

The best thing about free anti-spyware software is that it's free! If you don't want to pay for anti-spyware software, these free options are absolutely recommended. They can also be used as a backup for paid software to ensure that your system is as clean as possible (or to check that your paid software is doing a good job). Note that if you use multiple anti-spyware tools, one may list the other as spyware. For instance, many anti-spyware programs list Spybot Search&Destroy, a free anti-spyware program, as spyware.

The downside of free software is that you may lose out on other benefits, such as help desk support. In addition, some free anti-spyware software is written and maintained by one person or a small group of volunteers, which means that they may be slower to provide new signatures, new features, and software fixes than commercial products. You may also have to seek out and manually download new updates, whereas commercial products usually offer automatic updates.

The two most popular free anti-spyware products are Lavasoft's and Spybot Search&Destroy. Lavasoft also sells a commercial version of Ad-Aware, but Spybot is free (although you can make donations to its creator if you find the tool useful). Lavasoft and Spybot Search&Destroy both offer forums where you can post questions and find new information about the software.

In January 2005, Microsoft released a free anti-spyware tool called, cleverly enough, Microsoft AntiSpyware. The underlying program was acquired from GIANT Software Company. The software includes both scanning and preemptive blocking capabilities. You can also participate in the SpyNet community, a forum for collecting and reporting information about unwanted software.

Another well-known free tool is an anti-spyware scanner built into the Yahoo! toolbar. The spyware capability is only one feature; others include a pop-up blocker and links to other Yahoo! sites. If you download the toolbar you can get access to an anti-spyware community where you can post to a message board and get information about new spyware threats. Note that the anti-spyware scanner in the Yahoo! toolbar is based on Computer Associates' eTrust PestPatrol software.

Finally, you can download two useful free tools—HijackThis and CWShredder. HijackThis provides a log of your Registry, which you can use to detect unwanted programs such as browser hijackers. CWShredder is a tool to remove CoolWebSearch adware, which is a family of some of the Internet's most virulent and persistent malware. InterMute, the company that offers CWShredder for free download, has been acquired by Trend Micro. At the time I wrote this chapter, you could still find CWShredder at www.intermute.com/products/cwshredder.html. However, that may not be the case much longer. You may need to search www.trendmicro.com for the software, or download it from the Web site of Merijn Bellekom, who created CWShredder (and HijackThis). Table 5.4 lists this Web site and the sites of other free software.

What Anti-Spyware Software Can Do

Anti-spyware products scan your hard drive for unwanted software. When they detect that software, they ask you whether you want to delete it, quarantine it, or leave it alone. (Quarantining spyware leaves it on your computer but prevents it from operating.) Many products also perform proactive monitoring to ensure that unwanted programs aren't installed on your machine in the first place. For instance, Microsoft AntiSpyware includes components that monitor your applications and your computer's system settings in real time. It alerts you if attempts are made to change applications or settings. It also monitors programs on your computer that attempt to access the Internet.

Like the AV software discussed in Chapter 4, anti-spyware software uses signatures to detect malware on your computer. As you'll recall, a signature is

Table 5.4

Free Anti-Spyware Software		
Product	**Vendor**	**Web Site**
Ad-Aware SE Personal	Lavasoft	www.lavasoft.com
HijackThis and CWShredder[*]	Merijn/InterMute	www.merijn.org/downloads.html (for HijackThis and CWShredder) http://www.intermute.com/products/cwshredder.html (for CWShredder)
Microsoft AntiSpyware	Microsoft	www.microsoft.com
Spybot Search&Destroy	Safer-Networking	www.safer-networking.org
Yahoo! Toolbar with Anti-Spy	Yahoo!	http://toolbar.yahoo.com/ie

*HijackThis and CWShredder are not full anti-spyware solutions. HijackThis is a tool for manually removing browser hijackers. CWShredder is a removal tool only for CoolWebSearch, which has spawned an entire family of spyware variants. Also note that Web sites for Merijn, Lavasoft, and Spybot are sometimes victims of Denial of Service attacks or other attempts to take them offline. If you find these Web sites unavailable, try again later.

like a fingerprint of a specific piece of malware. Anti-spyware scans the files, registries, and programs on your hard drive, looking for these fingerprints. For anti-spyware software to be most effective, you must continually update the database of signatures. You must also scan your computer regularly to ensure that new spyware hasn't made its way to your computer. If you can, scan at least once a week.

You may also want to scan your computer before conducting sensitive transactions online, such as Web-based banking or other financial transactions. As discussed in Chapter 2, identity thieves try to plant spyware or Trojan horses on your computer to steal log-in information and passwords, or even piggyback on open sessions to make transactions of their own. You can feel more confident in your online transactions by running a scan first. Some companies have also started offering free malware scans to their customers before they engage in high-value transactions.

What Anti–Spyware Software Can't Do

Because anti-spyware software is signature-based, it requires a copy of known spyware to create a fingerprint. Like AV software, anti-spyware software is not guaranteed to prevent new spyware from infecting your computer.

Anti-spyware software does not offer complete protection from all classes of malware. While anti-spyware and AV products are beginning to overlap, anti-spyware software by itself is not sufficient protection from viruses, worms, and Trojan horses. In addition, anti-spyware products may not scan e-mail, which is becoming a popular infection vector for spyware. Deploy and run both AV and anti-spyware software for full protection.

Be Suspicious of Free Software

The Internet is crawling with free software, including games, file-sharing programs, screen savers, and so on. Some of it is quite harmless, and some of it is not. Companies often offer "free" software that includes adware or spyware. You should be suspicious of offers of free software. If the software doesn't include a EULA, privacy statement, and clear instructions on how to remove the software later, you may want to avoid downloading it.

Read the EULA

The End User License Agreement (EULA) is a contract between you and the software vendor. When you download and install software, you are presented with a screen that includes the EULA. The software does not allow you to continue installation until you click a button acknowledging that you've read and agreed to the terms of the agreement. Most people simply click the button without reading the license.

This is a mistake, especially with free software, because it often includes adware or other unwanted programs. Legitimate companies that offer free software inform you of the presence of adware somewhere in the EULA (probably toward the end) and give you the option of refusing the entire package. If you understand that accepting the free software means accepting the adware as well, you should proceed with the download.

If you've read the EULA and you found no mention of programs or functions that monitor your computer use, and then later you discover that the software did include unwanted programs, you can report the software provider to the FTC. The FTC is empowered to take action against companies that engage in deceptive practices. See the "Helpful Resources" section near the end of this chapter for information about filing complaints.

Adjust Your Browser Settings

You can adjust the IE browser's settings so that it warns you when an ActiveX control wants to be downloaded and so that it lets you accept or deny the download. To check the setting, open IE and select Tools and then Internet Options, and then click the Security tab. You see four Web zones for which you can adjust security settings: Internet, Local intranet, Trusted sites, and Restricted sites, as shown in Figure 5.4.

To change the settings for each zone, click the zone icon you want to adjust, and then click the Custom Level button. A new window called Security Settings opens, as shown in Figure 5.5. You can set individual rules for dealing with ActiveX controls, or simply choose the Medium setting near the bottom of the dialog box. As long as you've set the IE Security setting to Medium, you get a warning message; any other setting allows ActiveX controls to download without notification. (As mentioned, browser security is covered in greater detail in Chapter 7.)

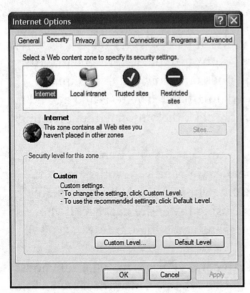

Figure 5.4   Internet Security options.

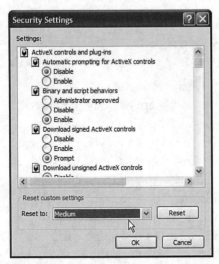

Figure 5.5   The Security Settings dialog box.

Unfortunately, even if a dialog box pops up to alert you of a download, click-ing No doesn't always help. Some malware writers manipulate the dialog box so that clicking No or any other button still downloads the software. Attackers may also try to disguise these pop-up messages to look like messages from your Windows PC as opposed to an ActiveX control, or make them appear to be generated by the Web site you're visiting. These messages are usually alarmist and prompt you to take some action immediately, such as clicking the Yes button to run a scan or download a program to repair the "problem." You should ignore these messages.

To close dialog boxes and pop-ups without clicking the No or Cancel button or the X in the upper-right corner, you can press Alt-F4. This safely closes windows inside a browser without allowing any downloads.

Use an Alternative Browser

Another option to help prevent spyware from being downloaded to your computer is to use a browser other than Internet Explorer. For instance, the Firefox and Opera browsers don't use ActiveX, which prevents ActiveX-based exploits from affecting your computer. These browsers are also less frequently subjected to vulnerability exploits (in part because they aren't nearly as widely used as Internet Explorer, and malware writers typically go after the most-used applications to infect as large an audience as possible). That said, alternative browsers are not invulnerable. (For example, from July to December 2004, there were 21 vulnerabilities affecting Mozilla browsers compared to 13 vulnerabilities affecting Microsoft Internet Explorer.) Therefore, if you do use one, you should check regularly for updates. You may also find that some Web sites don't work as well with alternative browsers.

To download the Firefox Web browser, go to www.mozilla.org. To download the Opera browser, go to www.opera.com.

Keep Your Software Updated

Updating your software is the computer equivalent of eating your vegetables: It is essential for good health, and you have to do it regularly. New spyware and adware programs are created all the time, as are the new signatures to detect them. Thus, it is important to update your security software. Most programs allow updates to be delivered automatically to you over the Internet.

The same applies for your operating system and application software. As noted earlier, Microsoft releases new updates, also called patches, on the second Tuesday of every month. Chapter 7 tells you how to set up your computer to get Microsoft updates automatically. Other vendors also release new software updates to address vulnerabilities that might allow an attacker to harm or commandeer your computer.

5.5 How to Remove Spyware, Adware, and Trojan Horses

If you follow all the preventative steps described here, you can keep most spyware and Trojan horses off your machine. But it's still possible that some program somewhere will slip past your defenses, so it's important to know the signs of infection and how to remove the unwanted software.

Your best bet for getting rid of unwanted software is to use anti-spyware and anti-virus tools. These tools search your computer for any traces of known spyware, adware, and Trojan horses. Once these traces are found, you can choose whether to delete, disable, or leave the programs alone. You can also remove spyware and Trojan horses manually, using tools available on the Internet.

How to Tell if Your Computer Is Infected

As with viruses and worms, the best way to tell if you've been infected with spyware, adware, or a Trojan horse is to use anti-spyware and anti-virus software. These programs detect the presence of unwanted software on your machine and provide you with options for dealing with it. You should regularly scan your computer with both kinds of software and also make sure that your security software is running while you surf the Internet.

If you don't already own anti-spyware software, you can get free scans from a variety of anti-spyware vendors. Webroot Software offers a free scan called Spy Audit, which can be found on the company's home page at www.webroot.com. Zone Labs at www.zonelabs.com, and Symantec at www.symantec.com, also offer spyware scans. Computer Associates offers a free scan at www.ca.com. Click the Products link under the Home and Home Office listing, and then click eTrust PestPatrol. That takes you to the page to run the scan. You can also get a free scan from Aluria Software by surfing to www.aluriasoftware.com. Many of these scans use an ActiveX control, so you have to click through a warning screen in your Internet Explorer browser.

You can also look for the following signs:

- Is your computer deluged with advertising?
- Does your Web home page keep changing even if you change it back?

- Are you directed to unfamiliar search sites that you didn't request?

- Is your computer sluggish, particularly when Web surfing? Spyware and adware that keep track of your activities use your Internet connection to send reports and direct advertising to your computer. This behavior steals bandwidth and affects the speed at which Web content gets delivered. Spyware and adware also use your computer's Central Processing Unit (CPU). If enough adware or spyware gets on your machine, this software competes for processing power with other applications and affects the over-all speed at which your computer performs normal functions. In many cases, infected computers simply become inoperable.

- Does your computer crash frequently?

- Do ads pop up on your computer even if you're not on the Internet?

- Do you see a new toolbar in your Web browser?

- Have you or someone who uses your computer downloaded "free" pro-grams such as file-sharing software, weather trackers, screen savers, or utili-ties that claim to enhance your online experience?

- Does your firewall detect programs on your computer trying to access the Internet?

Using HijackThis

To manually remove unwanted programs from your computer, you have to delete the files and Registry entries these programs create. This requires you to know what changes the spyware made to existing Registry keys and which new Registry keys it installed.

A popular tool for removing browser hijackers from the Registry is HijackThis. It scans your Registry and gives you a list (called a log) of the contents. You can then choose which of the contents to remove. You can find a copy of HijackThis at its creator's site: www.merijn.org/downloads.html. (He is also the creator of CWShredder, a popular removal tool for CoolWebSearch. CoolWebSearch is one of the most persistent and fast-evolving pieces of spyware on the Internet. CWShredder is available for free at www.merijn.org/downloads.html.)

HijackThis is a manual tool, meaning you have to remove unwanted content yourself. Unlike most commercial anti-spyware software, HijackThis doesn't offer advice on what you should and shouldn't remove. It is highly recommended that you get help in deciding which parts of the Registry to remove. If you make mistakes when changing your Registry, your computer may not work correctly. If you have a support contract with an AV or anti-spyware company or with your computer manufacturer, they may help you with a HijackThis log.

Alternatively, you can get free help with your HijackThis log at a number of online forums. These online forums are run by knowledgeable users who can help you review your log and make changes. One popular forum is CastleCops. Go to www.castlecops.com and click the Forums button near the top of the page, and then scroll down to the Privacy section and click the HijackThis - Spyware, Viruses, Worms, Trojans Oh My! entry, as shown in Figure 5.6. Be sure to read the guidelines for using the forum and posting HijackThis logs. CastleCops also has a technical tutorial on HijackThis at http://castlecops.com/HijackThis.html.

Figure 5.6 CastleCops' HijackThis Forum.

Another option is SpywareInfo, at www.spywareinfo.com. On the home page you can scroll down to look for a section called The Browser Hijacker Articles. The links in this section provide information on how to use HijackThis. You can also register to post your log or questions at a user forum. It also provides links to other online forums where you can review your HijackThis log.

You can also post logs at Spyware Warrior (www.spywarewarrior.com). Further listings to get assistance with HijackThis logs are at www.merijn.org.

Reformatting Your Hard Drive

In the worst-case scenario, the anti-spyware software won't be able to remove the unwanted programs, and you'll need to seek outside help. If you've purchased anti-spyware software, contact customer support to see what they recommend (but be prepared for a long wait). You can also contact your computer's manufacturer, seek help from the store where you bought the computer (for a fee, of course), or contact a local computer repair shop.

As a last resort, you might have to start from scratch and simply reinstall the operating system and applications using the original software discs. To do this, simply insert the original operating system disc into your CD drive and start the computer. The computer prompts you to reconfirm that you want to reinstall the operating system. However, reinstalling the operating system erases all the data you've saved on your computer (let's hope you have good backup habits). This is a last-ditch effort: exhaust other options before reformatting your hard drive.

5.6 Checklist

Use this checklist as a quick-reference guide to the material covered in this chapter.

Do

- Use anti-spyware software, and keep it updated.
- Adjust your browser settings to be notified of ActiveX downloads.
- Read the EULA before you download any software.
- Be suspicious of free software.
- Keep your application and operating system software updated.
- Perform regular backups of essential files.

Don't

- Accept unsolicited software downloads.
- Click pop-up ads or unsolicited and alarmist pop-ups that claim you have spyware or other problems with your PC.
- Accept e-mail attachments from strangers.

- Open e-mail that claims to come from a financial institution or e-commerce site that you don't do business with.
- Accept software without reading the EULA.
- Be afraid to try a new Web browser.

5.7 Helpful Resources

This section presents additional resources to help you learn more.

Ben Edelman is a law student at Harvard University and an anti-spyware researcher. His Web site is loaded with great information about deceptive practices of adware vendors, how programs exploit security holes, and critiques of anti-spyware legislation. You can read his postings at www.benedelman.org.

Spyware Warrior is an informative site about all things spyware, run by Eric Howes. If you're looking for a spyware product, check out the link that compares various anti-spyware software, including free products. The link to the Spyware blog takes you to a Web log with lots of current information about new spyware and developments in the anti-spyware community. You can also join various forums and post HijackThis logs. Go to www.spyware.com.

PC Pitstop offers diagnostic tools for PCs and also provides useful information about spyware. For instance, check out its ranking of the top 25 spyware and adware programs at http://www.pcpitstop.com/spycheck/top25.asp.

Merijn Bellekom is the author of HijackThis, CWShredder, and other useful anti-spyware tools, all of which you can download at www.merijn.org.

Spywareinfo.com is chock full of good information. If you'd like to learn more about spyware, cookies, browser hijacking, and more, click the More Links button on the opening page. It also recommends products to help you deal with unwanted software. If you register at the site, you can post questions to a message board and get assistance with spyware problems (just be sure to read the FAQ first). You can also subscribe to the newsletter, written by Mike Healan, the site's creator.

To read a copy of the FTC's March 2005 report on spyware, go to www.ftc.gov/os/2005/03/050307spywarerpt.pdf. To file a compliant about spyware or adware with the FTC, go to www.ftc.gov and click the File a Complaint link on the opening page. You can also call 877-FTC-HELP (877-382-4357).

Spywareguide.com has a searchable database of known spyware and adware. You can enter a program's name into the search bar on the home page to see if the program is listed. The site also ranks spyware programs according to a danger level of 1 through 10, with descriptions of each level.

Reading the Fine Print

Kazaa, which makes peer-to-peer software for sharing files over the Internet, includes adware in the free version of its product. Of course, the software is free because you agree to have adware generate targeted advertising.

The company explains this in its EULA, which you can read at www.kazaa. com/us/terms2.htm. The sections on adware are listed toward the bottom of the EULA in Section 9. As of mid-2005, Kazaa bundled five adware programs, including Cydoor, an advertising delivery program that, according to the Kazaa EULA, "uses your Internet connection to update its selection of available ads and stores them on your hard drive."

It also includes the GAIN AdServer, which, according to the Kazaa EULA, "identifies your interests based on some of your computer usage and uses that information to deliver advertising messages to you."

The Kazaa EULA also includes links to the EULAs for Cydoor and GAIN AdServer and says that by downloading Kazaa you basically acknowledge and accept the EULAs for each of these software components.

In addition, the EULA states that you will not use any other software to disable or block any of the ads that are served by these components. If you remove any of these components, Kazaa ceases to function.

So what should you do if you really want the free file-sharing software? You have to decide about the trade-offs. As long as you're willing to accept the consequences that come with adware (annoying ads, potentially poorer performance on your PC, and whatever vulnerabilities are introduced by having adware on your computer), you can download the software and start sharing files.

Chapter 6

Just Say No to Spam

Spam has one purpose: to generate income for those of dubious moral fiber. As with high-risk adware and spyware, fighting spam is difficult because spammers have a financial incentive to persist and innovate. The result is an ongoing game of one-upmanship between pro- and anti-spam factions. On the one hand, spammers try everything: manipulation of e-mail systems, technologically sophisticated attempts to defeat spam filters, and brute-force floods of junk mail that try to overwhelm defenses by sheer volume. On the other hand, new technologies are being developed and refined to thwart junk mail, laws are being enforced to pursue and prosecute spammers, and consumers are getting smarter about dealing with it.

In the days when the Internet began to attract a widespread consumer audience, spam severely crippled e-mail and nearly killed it. Today, for most home consumers, spam is an annoyance rather than a plague. Thanks to the efforts of software developers, service providers, and a vigorous anti-spam community, most spam gets filtered at a gateway and never makes it into your inbox. Internet service providers (ISPs) such as AOL and Comcast, and Web mail providers like Yahoo!, MSN, and Google, ensure that their users get a fairly clean mail stream. Questionable messages are forwarded to bulk mail folders for you to review, and patently obvious spam is killed without being delivered.

That said, spam shows no signs of letting up. For every advance in anti-spam technology comes a counter-advance in mass-mailing techniques. Approximately 30 billion e-mails a day are sent across the Internet, and conservative estimates say that at least 50 percent of those e-mails are spam. (Other estimates put spam at 90 percent of all e-mail.) You might think that's of little concern to you as long as that junk e-mail never makes it to your inbox. In fact, 15 billion (or more) junk messages create significant costs for carriers and service providers. Each junk message that traverses the Internet eats up resources, such as bandwidth on fiber-optic lines and the processing capabilities of the routers and mail servers that pass messages from one hop to the next. Carriers and service providers also must invest in software to process and analyze incoming messages, and they must purchase ever-greater amounts of hardware to handle the volume of mail. Those costs are passed along to you in the form of higher monthly fees.

Mass-mailing techniques are also being adopted by virus and malware writers, who are always looking for new ways to increase the spread of their insidious creations. A new version of spam called phishing sends bulk e-mail to trick people into divulging bank account information. Thus, spam is no longer simply annoying: It also can be dangerous.

And the problem will never go away as long as two conditions exist. First, it's still easy for spammers to hide. Thanks to e-mail obfuscation techniques, spammers can disguise the source of their junk mail. The Internet is also full of unsecured machines, whether mail servers or home computers, which spammers can hijack and use as unwitting spam generators. Also, the world is full of service providers that are willing to look the other way concerning customers who generate thousands or hundreds of thousands of messages a day—as long as their checks keep clearing.

Second, spam will persist as long as gullible people respond and actually purchase the products and services advertised or fall victim to the scams being propagated. This chapter includes a brief primer on the economics of spam, information on how spammers operate and the tools anti-spammers use, a section on the inner workings of the e-mail infrastructure, and useful tips to ensure that you don't become a junk-mail casualty. We'll also look at several products that can help keep spam from reaching your desktop.

6.1 Spamonomics

Spam is a money game and thus obeys simple economic principles: As long as the income derived from spam is greater than the cost of sending it, spam will persist. As a form of advertising, spam is the cheapest there is. If you wanted to sell magic weight-loss pills via any other medium, you'd have to bear significant up-front expenses to pay for advertising. But sending 100,000 e-mails a day costs little more than an Internet connection, a few computers, and some prepackaged spam software (yes, you can buy spam software—on the Internet, of course).

Spammers can make good money. Take the case of junk e-mailer Jeremy Jaynes. He was sentenced to nine years in jail in November 2004 for sending a large volume of unsolicited e-mail and falsifying the routing information on the e-mail messages to prevent recipients from identifying the sender. Jaynes ran several kinds of spam pitches, including pornography, privacy software, a penny stock-picking service, and a work-from-home scheme. According to court documents, Jaynes' bulk-mailing operations generated approximately 10,000 credit card sales per month. And although a full two-thirds of those who bought a product requested their money back, Jaynes still netted a profit of more than $100,000 a month. Prosecutors estimated Jaynes' overall net worth at approximately $24 million.

Of course, for spamonomics to be successful, there must be buyers as well as sellers. The only reason that spam persists is that someone, somewhere, actually buys something advertised via junk mail. This element may be the one unsolvable aspect of the spam problem. Spam filtering software can be continually refined, but it seems that human gullibility (or just plain stupidity) is a persistent glitch. In fact, the number of people who respond to spam may be higher than you think. In 2004, a study by the Pew Internet & American Life Project found that 5 percent of Internet users had purchased a product advertised in an unsolicited e-mail. In the same year the Business Software Alliance released the results of a survey that found that 21 percent of U.S. survey respondents purchased something from a spam advertisement.

So what makes people respond to spam offers? I'm not a psychologist, but here are a couple of theories:

- Spam appeals to base human desires. Spam usually addresses three desires: sex (porn, Viagra), money (pyramid schemes, cheap mortgages, cheap software, Nigerian oil money schemes), and an improved self-image (weight loss, penis enlargement, and cheap knock-offs of prestige design-er items). In fact, the buttons that spammers try to push aren't so differ-ent from the ones that mainstream advertisers use. Both spammers and Madison Avenue profit from our preoccupation with our finances, self-image, and sexual prowess. What makes spammers different is that they advertise on the cheap, they are harder to track down, their methods are often illegal, and they are certainly more likely to rip you off.

- Spam provides a measure of anonymity. A person embarrassed to buy pornography or a penis enlargement kit at a store may find the pseudo-anonymity of the Internet appealing. Someone who doesn't want to ask his doctor for a Viagra prescription can self-medicate thanks to spam. A person who wouldn't buy counterfeit software out of someone's trunk might feel more comfortable doing it over the Internet. The solitary computer screen and the seemingly ethereal medium of Internet communications can sub-vert the sense of public shame that bolsters (or substitutes for) our better nature.

6.2 Spam, Scams, and Phishing

While traditional spam continues to exist (by traditional I mean unsolicited e-mail that tries to sell you something), criminals also rely on variants of spam to trick unsuspecting recipients into falling for various scams. The best-known is the Nigerian oil scam, in which a correspondent claims to have millions of dollars that he is trying to transfer out of Africa. (This category is sometimes called 419 scams after the Nigerian penal code.) The sender promises to transfer a generous share of the money to your bank account, but before that happens, you need to send money for various "fees" and other issues. Another popular e-mail scam is an international lottery—you can collect your winnings after you pay a small administrative fee (and hell freezes over). The gist of this kind of scam (and there are dozens of variants) is that you think you will get something for nothing. The truth is quite the opposite.

The second and potentially more dangerous spam variant is called phishing. Chapter 2, "Preventing Identity Theft," covered phishing, but we'll review it here in case you skipped that chapter.

Phishing attacks start with an e-mail (sent in bulk) that claims to be from a bank, credit card company, ISP, or e-commerce company (eBay and PayPal are two popular targets). Some phishing e-mail is an obvious scam, but other messages are a work of art, complete with the company logo and written in the language of corporate marketing. Figure 6.1 is a good example of the latter.

From:	"PayPal" <service@paypal.com> 🗐 Add to Address Book
To:	aconrymurray@yahoo.com
Subject:	PayPal Account Security Measures
Date:	Tue, 15 Feb 05 22:25:54 GMT

Dear PayPal Member,

Your account has been randomly flagged in our system as a part of our routine security measures. This is a must to ensure that only you have access and use of your PayPal account and to ensure a safe PayPal experience. We require all flagged accounts to verify their information on file with us. To verify your information at this time, please visit our secure server webform by clicking the hyperlink below.

Click here to verify your Information

Thank you for using PayPal!
The PayPal Team

Please do not reply to this e-mail. Mail sent to this address cannot be answered. For assistance, log in to your PayPal account and choose the "Help" link in the footer of any page.

Protect Your Account Info

Make sure you never provide your password to fraudulent websites.

To safely and securely access the PayPal website or your account, open up a new web browser (e.g. Internet Explorer or Netscape) and type in the PayPal URL (http://www.paypal.com/).

PayPal will never ask you to enter your password in an email.

For more information on protecting yourself from fraud, please review our Security Tips at http://www.paypal.com/securitytips

Figure 6.1   A phony PayPal e-mail.

In general, phishing e-mail contains an alarming message that says something is wrong with your account and it must be dealt with immediately. The e-mail includes what looks like a link to the Web site's sign-in page. If you click the link, you'll find a log-on page that looks identical to the regular site, complete with fields to enter your username, account number, and password. Many spoofed sites get greedy and ask for other information, like your Social Security number. You, the victim, wanting to address any problems with your account, dutifully type in the information and click Send. Your information has just been stolen.

As if this weren't bad enough, phishers are getting more clever. Many are including malicious software programs in the e-mail they send or on the web site they send you to, such as viruses, keystroke loggers, or Trojan horses (see Chapters 4, "Getting Rid of Unwanted Guests, Part 1," and 5, "Getting Rid of Unwanted Guests, Part 2"). In some cases, simply opening the e-mail is sufficient for the malware to load itself onto your computer. Thus, even if you don't fall for the phishing scam itself, your computer may still get infected.

6.3 How Spammers Operate

Spammers use a variety of methods to ply their trade. Some of these methods are technically sophisticated and involve manipulating the Internet protocols used to deliver and track e-mail. Others are as simple as buying a CD of e-mail addresses. Spammers always operate in bulk because of the difficulty of getting a spam message through the various filters that are erected by service providers and end users. Thus, a spammer sends millions of messages in the hopes that 1 or 2 percent will find their way into an inbox and that a further 1 or 2 percent will actually generate a sale. This section looks at some of the most common tricks of the trade.

Buying Lists

The simplest way to get started is to buy lists of e-mail addresses. For instance, a company called Bulk Email Software Superstore will sell you one million e-mail addresses for $40. A simple Internet search will call up dozens of sites with similar offers. Spammers can also buy lists of stolen e-mail addresses. In June 2004, a software engineer at AOL was charged with stealing up to 92 million e-mail addresses of AOL users, which he resold to spammers.

E-Mail Scavengers

Programs are available on the Internet that crawl Web pages looking for e-mail addresses. These scavengers or crawlers scan millions of pages, looking for the telltale @ sign and building a database of e-mail addresses. Spammers and companies that sell products to spammers use these crawlers as a way to accumulate addresses.

Dictionary Attack/Directory Harvesting

A dictionary attack (also known as directory harvesting) is an inelegant, brute-force approach to sending spam. The spammer simply creates a program that cycles through variants of common names (John_Smith@isp.com, J_Smith@isp. com, jsmith@isp.com, Ted_Smith@isp.com), chooses a particular domain as a target, and fires up the program. The program then sends hundreds of thousands or millions of e-mails in the hopes that it will hit upon enough legitimate combinations of names to get the message delivered. Dictionary attacks are a serious problem because they can overwhelm a target mail server and use up computing resources so much that legitimate mail can't get through.

Spoofing

Spammers try everything they can to hide a message's origins because service providers are moving more quickly to block spam sources and because the federal CAN-SPAM act means that spammers can be sent to jail if they are caught and prosecuted.

As mentioned earlier, SMTP is the protocol for sending e-mail. SMTP relies on two kinds of headers when delivering mail: envelope headers and message headers. SMTP uses envelope headers to tell intervening mail servers where to send the message. Each mail server the e-mail passes through also adds its own message headers. By reading envelope headers, you can see the progress an e-mail made through the Internet. However, spammers can also create fake headers and inject e-mail messages into mail server relays to help hide their tracks.

Message headers include the To: and From: lines that you see in your e-mail client. These message headers are easy to forge. You can do it yourself by simply putting a bogus e-mail address into the From: line.

Spam Proxies

Spam proxies are mail servers or PCs that have been hijacked to send spam. A spam proxy may be a mail server that is misconfigured as an open relay. In other cases, spammers try to plant Trojan horse programs on PCs. As explained in Chapter 5, Trojan horse programs pose as innocent or useful pieces of software, but when installed they can give an attacker complete control over a computer. For example, in August 2003 the "F" variant of the SoBig virus included a Trojan horse that allowed spammers to turn the compromised computer into a spam relay. PCs with broadband connections are popular targets for spam proxy attacks because of their high-bandwidth, always-on Internet connections.

Spam proxies are valuable to spammers. They mask the true origin of the spam e-mail, and once the spam proxy gets blacklisted (that is, ISPs stop accepting mail from the device), the spammers simply abandon the blacklisted proxies and "recruit" new ones.

Social Engineering

Once a spammer has an e-mail address, he or she needs to craft an appealing or enticing message to get you to open it. This is where social engineering comes into play. Social engineering is just a fancy way to describe tricking people. Some spam messages don't bother with social engineering—they want you to know it's an offer to buy Viagra. Other spammers want you to open and read the e-mail, so they use enticing or deliberately vague subject headers (such as Hello!). Phishing e-mail relies heavily on social engineering because the scam falls apart if you don't believe it comes from the organization it claims to come from.

Web Beacons/Web Bugs

Web beacons, also known as Web bugs, are tiny pieces of code such as HTML or a GIF (an image file). When it's activated, a Web beacon opens a connection to a server to download an image file. At the same time, the Web beacon can also transmit information to the Web server. Web beacons can be placed on a Web page or in an e-mail to track user behavior. Many legitimate Web sites use Web beacons in combination with cookies to analyze user behavior and help personalize the browsing experience. Spammers place Web beacons inside a spam message to find out if the message has been opened. This helps spammers sort out "live" addresses from unresponsive ones. Web beacons can be as small as a single pixel, making them impossible to detect with the human eye.

6.4 Spam Filtering Methods

Necessity is the mother of invention, and that's clearly the case with anti-spam filters. In the years that anti-spam researchers have been fighting their battles, filtering methods have grown from simple keyword searches to complex statistical analysis tools with grounding in artificial intelligence research. The result is a comprehensive toolbox that anti-spam products draw on to help them detect and remove spam.

All these tools are automated; that is, a computer program inspects incoming messages and decides whether they are spam or ham ("ham" means wanted messages). However, every anti-spam filtering tool risks misidentifying a message. There are two ways to incorrectly identify a message. Labeling a wanted message as spam is called a false positive. Labeling a spam message as ham is called a false negative. Mislabeling has consequences that you, the end user, need to be aware of. The consequence of a false negative is merely that a spam message gets delivered to your inbox. The consequence of a false positive is that a good message never gets delivered to you.

The filtering methods discussed here can usually be tweaked to find a balance between maximizing spam detection while minimizing false positives. Major e-mail providers such as Yahoo! and AOL tend to be slightly more conservative; that is, they risk delivering a slightly higher percentage of spam e-mail to ensure that no legitimate messages get lost. This is why most mail providers hedge their bets by using a bulk mail folder. Messages that the computer can't definitively categorize are routed here so that you can make the final judgment.

The technologies listed in the rest of this section are generally used by service providers, businesses, and administrators of small mail servers. Some of them are also finding their way into anti-spam products for consumers. If you are implementing a personal mail filter for your desktop e-mail client, this list can help you understand the tools being used to help weed out spam.

Content Filters/Keyword Searches

Keyword searches scan subject lines and message bodies for words and word combinations that indicate a message is spam. Keyword searching is one of the oldest and most obvious methods of fighting spam. It's also one of the least effective.

While word searches give you very granular control over word lists, the danger of false positives is high. For instance, if the word "breast" is forbidden, a keyword search might block e-mail about breast cancer research or other harmless topics. Word searches are also easy for spammers to get around. Many spam tools can intentionally misspell words that fool a filter but that the human brain can still comprehend, such as spelling "porn" with a zero instead of an "o" (p0rn). Getting around keyword filters also accounts for the incredible number of variations of the word Viagra. There are numerous ways to manipulate the spelling of Viagra—too many to make a database of all those variations worth loading onto a mail server. Spam tools can also perform other tricks, like inserting HTML comments between the letters of a word. While the HTML isn't visible to the person reading the word, it fools the filter.

Blacklists

Blacklists block e-mail that comes from specific IP addresses or domains. A well-maintained blacklist can be very effective at blocking known sources of spam. The most famous blacklist is the Mail Abuse Prevention System (MAPS, www.mail-abuse.com). Its Realtime Blackhole List (RBL) is a database of IP addresses of mail servers known to be friendly, or at least neutral, to spammers. Other well-known blacklists are maintained at SpamCop (www.spamcop.net) and SpamHause (www.spamhause.org). These blacklists are used by service providers, businesses, and anyone running a mail server. Your ISP may use these or other blacklist sources as part of its spam-filtering service.

However, blacklists can be a blunt instrument. Spammers constantly change IP addresses and domains, so a blacklist can quickly become out of date. In addition, a compromised computer or mail server that gets onto a blacklist might have a hard time getting off once the problem is resolved. In the meantime, any organization using the database continues blocking e-mail even if it isn't spam. If you find a consumer-oriented blacklist, be sure to check out the criteria for adding domains and IP addresses to the list, how quickly domains can be removed, and how often the list is updated.

White Lists

White lists are collections of trusted e-mail addresses or domains. White listing is very accurate and complements blacklists by providing more granular control. While a blacklist can block a general domain, the white list can open up portions of that domain known to send wanted mail. White listing is also useful because it ensures mail delivery from trusted sources and lets those messages bypass other spam detection methods, saving both time and processing power. On the downside, white lists need constant maintenance as addresses or domains get added or removed.

Heuristics Analysis

Heuristics analysis runs incoming messages through a variety of tests. These tests search for characteristics that are likely indicators of spam. Each characteristic is assigned a spam probability, and the message is given a cumulative probability score based on the test results. For example, to get around keyword filtering, some spammers embed images or HTML references in the message body. When you open the mail (often disguised with an innocuous or misleading subject line), your e-mail client displays the image. As you might imagine (or have seen), many of these images are sexually explicit. A heuristics analysis filter might use image detection as one of the checks. When combined with other checks, such as a message that includes large-point fonts, randomly inserted text, and forged headers, that message gets a higher probability rating than a message that says "mortgage rates" but otherwise triggers no alarms. By weighing a variety of characteristics, heuristics analysis increases the confidence that a message with a high spam score is actually junk mail (and vice versa). A popular heuristics filtering tool for mail servers is the open-source SpamAssassin (http://spamassassin.apache.org/).

However, heuristics can still generate false positives. In addition, new tests need to be created to counter novel spam techniques, and older tests must be phased out as they become obsolete. Your service provider probably uses heuristics analysis as part of its spam filtering toolkit. Desktop anti-spam software may also use heuristics analysis.

Spam Signatures

This method borrows a page from the anti-virus (AV) playbook and is a popular anti-spam technique. A computer program derives the checksum or cryptographic hash of a known spam message, which creates a signature or fingerprint of that message. A checksum or hash is a mathematical operation that can turn a text-based message into a numeric sum. If you run a checksum on two identical copies of a message, you arrive at the same sum. Any change to the text of the message generates a different sum. Checksums turn out to be great for identifying spam because spammers send thousands or millions of the same message. A signature-based filter keeps a copy of the signature of current spam messages and then runs a checksum operation on incoming messages. Any incoming messages that match a signature are guaranteed to be spam and can be discarded.

However, spammers have discovered workarounds to this technique. For instance, many spam tools insert random strings of letters and numbers at the end of the subject line or within the body of each message sent. They also insert HTML comments between words and letters. They are invisible to the human recipient but would be included in any checksum function. Placing random elements within the e-mail ensures that a checksum operation produces a different value for messages that are otherwise identical.

Of course, the anti-spam community is fighting back by using prefilters to screen out random insertions and creating checksums only for the most significant characteristics of a message. The greatest constraint on spam signature techniques is time: A signature isn't any good to you if the spam hits your inbox before the signature hits the database.

Challenge/Response

A challenge/response system exploits the fact that spam is automated by quarantining mail from new senders and requesting that the sender complete a challenge. If there's a human at the other end, he or she responds to the challenge, and the original message is allowed to enter your inbox. If the message came from a spammer, the From: address is probably forged anyway, so the challenge is not acknowledged. Even if the spammer's From: address is valid, it likely was mailed by a computer program and therefore won't know how to respond to the challenge. Either way, the sender fails the challenge, and the associated mail gets discarded.

The challenge is usually some kind of puzzle or test that can be solved only by a human. One popular challenge is to display letters or numbers that are warped or slightly obfuscated but that can still be made out by a person. The person then has to send back the correct response to the challenge.

The major problem with the challenge/response mechanism is that it can generate lots of additional mail traffic, which is counterproductive for service providers and businesses that are trying to reduce the volume of e-mail being generated. Legitimate e-mail may also be discarded if the sender doesn't reply to the challenge e-mail within a specified time.

Bayesian Filtering

Bayesian filtering is a form of text classification that can be applied to spam detection. A Bayesian filter "learns" to differentiate spam from nonspam by examining the language used in a set of spam messages and the language used in a set of regular messages. For instance, the phrase "click here" may appear in 90 out of 100 spam mails. The filter assigns a very high probability to "click here" as indicative of spam. On the other hand, "Area 51" may appear in the majority of a UFO junkie's nonspam e-mails. In this case, the filter assigns a high probability that the presence of "Area 51" indicates a nonspam message.

As new messages come in, the filter rounds up the words or phrases that have the highest probabilities in either direction—spam or not spam. Then the filter calculates a new probability that the message is spam or is not spam using the individual scores of the collected words.

Bayesian filtering is garnering attention for its spectacular detection rates. Bill Yerazunis, creator of a filter called CRM114 (http://crm114.sourceforge.net), claims a greater than 99.9 percent accuracy on his own incoming e-mails. Paul Graham, a Bayesian filter creator, claims a detection rate of 99.75 percent in a one-month period. He also reported eight false positives out of more than 7,000 legitimate messages in that time. His essay, "A Plan for Spam," describes Bayesian filtering in more detail at http://www.paulgraham.com/spam.html.

Bayesian filters work best when they are trained by individual users on their own bodies of spam and nonspam e-mail. Note that a Bayesian filter must be retrained regularly to adapt to changes in spam. Without retraining, its performance degrades. Spammers also engage in Bayesian poisoning, in which they include large chunks of random text, such as a passage from an encyclopedia, to try to skew the message content toward a nonspam rating.

Reputation Filtering

Several companies now track IP addresses and domains and give them a reputation score based on the amount of good e-mail and spam e-mail they send. Mail servers can then be configured to block e-mail from any sources that have a poor reputation. This is somewhat like blacklisting, except reputation filters can be more flexible. For instance, an IP address or domain can be removed from a reputation filter more quickly once its behavior begins to change.

A company called Cloudmark relies on user opinions to separate spam from ham. If Cloudmark subscribers receive a message they think is spam, they report that message back to Cloudmark, which creates a fingerprint of it. The service then weighs the user's reputation for accuracy to decide if Cloudmark should block the message for the rest of the community. Cloudmark says it has more than a million users in its community. If you use Microsoft Outlook or Outlook Express, you can try the service for free at www.cloudmark.com/safetybar/.

Another take on reputation filtering is the Bonded Sender program. Organizations that send bulk commercial e-mail that customers have requested (such as newsletters, financial statements, and so on) often find that their messages get blocked by spam filters. To help legitimate commercial mail navigate spam filters, these organizations can put down a financial bond through the

Bonded Sender program. If an end user complains that the e-mail was in fact unsolicited, the organization suffers a financial penalty that comes out of the bond money. In return for this guarantee, spam filter owners can allow e-mail from Bonded Sender participants to bypass their filters. The Bonded Sender program is sponsored by IronPort, which makes e-mail servers. Individual users can't join the program, but you can find out more about it at www.bondedsender.com.

6.5 How to Reduce Spam

There are numerous ways to make sure your inbox doesn't get overwhelmed with spam. This section outlines simple techniques you can use that don't cost any money. Most of them involve a healthy dose of common sense. In general, treat your e-mail address the same way you treat other sensitive information, like your phone number. These tips won't eliminate spam, but they can help keep the volume to a manageable level.

Delete Suspicious E-Mail Without Opening It

It's possible to spot spam, phishing, or fraudulent e-mails by information in the e-mail address or subject line. The following list can help you identify unwanted mail. If you are suspicious of an e-mail, your best bet is to delete it without opening it. Many spam messages use Web beacons, as described earlier, to detect live mail. By opening a message, you active the beacon, and your e-mail increases in value to a spammer. Many phishing e-mails now carry viruses or other malware that can attack your computer simply by your opening the e-mail. Thus, the safest bet is to delete suspicious messages without reading them.

Here are some tips to spot spam and phishing e-mail without opening the message:

- The e-mail address is one you've never seen before.
- The e-mail domain comes from a foreign country that you don't have interactions with.
- The text in the Subject line has odd spellings or strange characters (such as V1AGR@).
- The text of the Subject line uses vague but compelling language (for instance, "Urgent!", "Important Notification!", or "INVITATION").

- The text of the Subject line indicates some kind of offer, proposal, sales pitch, or business transaction.
- The text of the Subject line uses "Re:" and vague language such as "Your document" or "As we discussed" to make it appear to be a response to a message you've sent. If you don't recognize the e-mail address or the context of the conversation, it's probably a trick.
- The e-mail claims to be from a bank or e-commerce site that you don't do business with.

Don't Reply to Spam or Phishing Mail

If you do open a message and it turns out to be spam, don't reply. Replying merely informs the spammer that he's reached a live address. Some spam messages also claim to have an opt-out policy; that is, you can write back to say that you don't want to receive further messages. Most often this is a trick. If you opt out, the spammer knows that he or she has reached a live address.

Don't Click Any Links in Untrusted Mail

If you've opened an e-mail and you're still not sure if it's for real, don't click any links included in the message. These links may activate malware or take you to a mock Web site. If you really want to investigate the offer, close the message, open your Web browser, and manually type the address into the URL field. You can also check the Anti-Phishing Working Group's (APWG) Web site. The APWG is an organization working to create industry best practices for addressing phishing attacks. The group is creating a database of phishing messages to help consumers identify scam e-mails. You can find the collection of phishing messages by surfing to www.antiphishing.org and clicking the Phishing Archive link on the left side of the page.

Read Privacy Policies

Before doing business with an e-commerce site, it's best to read the privacy policy to find out what kind of information it will collect from you (most sites require an e-mail address) and what it will do with that information. Legitimate businesses should provide a clear link to the privacy policy on their Web sites. They should also provide you with an opportunity to opt out of receiving unsolicited e-mail and from having the company sell your information to other businesses.

Don't Post Your E-Mail Address

If you frequent chat rooms or post messages on discussion boards or blogs, don't include your e-mail address. Also, if you have your own Web site, don't post your e-mail address on it. Spammers use automated programs to crawl the Internet and harvest e-mail addresses (often by looking for the @ symbol).

Alter Your E-Mail or Use Multiple E-Mail Addresses

If you do want to post your e-mail address, you can alter it to thwart automated crawlers. The two most common tricks are to write out the @ symbol and the period (johndoe at isp dot com) or to add a phrase like "no spam" in the address (janedoe@nospam.isp.com). Any crawler that picks up this address won't be able to deliver messages to it, but humans should know enough to leave out the phrase when sending a message. (If you're worried that people will think "no spam" is part of the address, you can include instructions on the Web page.)

However, spam programs are likely to refine their tools enough to detect tricks like this, so another option is to use multiple e-mails. For instance, you can set up an address that you give out to only family and friends. Then you can create additional accounts to use in public, whether for posting online or when dealing with sites that you suspect might trade or sell your e-mail.

Another option is to choose a nonobvious e-mail address. For instance, instead of using some combination of your first and last name (johndoe@isp.com), try a combination of letters and numbers, or a phrase (for instance, j225doe@isp.com or dontpanic@isp.com). This can help prevent dictionary spam (although it also may make it harder for you to remember your address).

Additionally, some mail services allow you to create "disposable" addresses. For instance, Yahoo! Mail Plus lets you create as many as 500 addresses within your Yahoo account (this option is not available with a free Yahoo! Mail account). You can use the disposable addresses for dealing with e-commerce sites, posting on message boards, and so on. If a disposable address begins receiving large amounts of spam, you can simply deactivate it so that no more messages that use that address are delivered to you. You can check with your ISP or Web mail provider to see if it offers a similar feature.

Don't Buy Anything from Spammers

If everyone in the world followed this step, spam would cease to exist. Unfortunately, the world is filled with a sufficient number of people who are either gullible or intrigued enough to purchase something advertised via spam. Thus, we'll likely have to rely on technological solutions until the day that being an idiot can be corrected by surgery.

Report Spam and Phishing

You can report spam and phishing e-mails to a variety of organizations, including your service provider, the government, and anti-spam/anti-phishing organizations. By reporting spam, you help your service provider refine its spam detection capabilities; your report may also provide more evidence if the provider decides to take legal action against a spammer. Check with your service provider about the steps it prefers for reporting spam. A free service called SpamCop can report spam for you and add the source of the spam to a blocking list. You need to register at the Web site (www.spamcop.net), and your e-mail client needs to be able to display the full message headers (not just the To: and From: headers). Check with your e-mail software FAQ to find out how to reveal the full headers.

You can also report spam and phishing e-mails to the Federal Trade Commission. The FTC is accumulating spam e-mails to use in pursuing legal action against spammers. You can send spam e-mail to spam@uce.gov. (UCE stands for Unsolicited Commercial E-mail, a more polite term for spam.)

Last, you can send phishing e-mails to the Anti-Phishing Working Group. The APWG prefers that people not forward the phishing messages. Instead, open a new message addressed to reportphishing@antiphishing.org, paste the phishing message into the new message, and send it.

6.6 Anti-Spam Tools

At a technological level, the war on spam is being fought primarily by service providers and the administrators of corporate and personal e-mail servers. It's generally invisible to consumers (except when errant spam messages make it through to your inbox). Most service providers do allow customers some amount of customization. For instance, AOL lets subscribers create their own blacklists and white lists, use keyword filtering, and block images included in messages from unknown senders. Yahoo! lets users create blacklists and block images and Web beacons. Earthlink lets users block any mail from senders that aren't in their personal address books (an extreme form of white listing).

Software is also available for consumers who want to apply additional spam controls to their home computers. Table 6.1 outlines a few options. A simple Web search for "anti-spam software" or "spam filters" can also direct you to considerably more choices. Computer magazines and online Web reviews of anti-spam products are also available from *PC Magazine* (www.pcmagazine.com), *PC World* (www.pcworld.com), and CNET (www.cnet.com). As of mid-2005, prices ranged from $29.95 to $39.95 for standalone anti-spam software, and from $49.95 to $79.95 for security suites that include anti-spam along with other essential software including anti-virus, anti-spyware, and a firewall. Note that special offers and rebates may affect the final cost.

Table 6.1

Selected Anti-Spam Products			
Product	**Vendor**	**Web Site**	**Features**
Anti-Spam Personal	Kaspersky Lab	www.kaspersky.com	Not available at press time.
Cloudmark SafetyBar 4.0	Cloudmark	www.cloudmark.com	Defines spam based on feedback from more than a million users. For Outlook and Outlook Express.
MailFrontier Desktop	MailFrontier	www.mailfrontier.com	Blacklists, white lists, phishing and fraud detection, user feedback, challenge/response options. For Outlook and Outlook Express, Hotmail, and MSN.
Norton AntiSpam	Symantec	www.symantec.com	Blacklist, white list (synchronizes with your Outlook, Outlook Express, or Eudora address book), filters spam from Yahoo! Web mail, can block e-mail in foreign languages.

Product	Vendor	Web Site	Features
OnlyMyEmail Personal	OnlyMyEmail	www.onlymyemail.com	Service-based. Multiple analysis engines, blacklists, white lists. For Outlook, Outlook Express, and Web mail.
Panda Platinum Internet Security 2005	Panda Software	www.pandasoftware.com	Analysis engine, white lists, phishing detection. For Outlook and Outlook Express.
PC-cillin Internet Security	Trend Micro	www.trendmicro.com	Can filter spam for Outlook Express, AOL, Yahoo!, MSN Hotmail, and Eudora.
Spam Filter Express	ANVSOFT	www.spam-filter-express.com	Bayesian filtering, black lists, white lists. For Outlook and Outlook Express.
SpamKiller	McAfee	www.mcafee.com	Includes blacklists, white lists, spam signatures, Bayesian filtering, image filtering, and foreign language filtering.
ZoneAlarm Security Suite	Zone Labs	www.zonelabs.com	Routes spam to three folders: challenged mail, junk mail, and fraudulent mail.

6.7 Checklist

Use this checklist as a quick-reference guide to the material covered in this chapter.

Do

- Delete suspicious messages without opening them first.
- Read privacy policies.
- Keep your e-mail address as private as possible.
- Report spam and phishing to the FTC and the Anti-Phishing Working Group.

Don't

- Click links inside suspicious-sounding messages.
- Post your e-mail address online.
- Buy anything from a spammer.
- Be swayed by alarmist e-mails demanding immediate action.

6.8 Helpful Resources

This section presents additional resources to help you learn more.

Spamroll is a blog about all things spammy. It covers news from the world of spam, provides information about spam and phishing, and includes an archive of spam messages. You can even contribute your own spam to the archive. Check it out at www.spamroll.com.

You can use SpamCop to help report spam to your service provider. SpamCop also maintains a blacklist for service providers and e-mail administrators. Check it out at www.spamcop.net.

David Sorkin tracks spam legislation for U.S. state and federal laws, as well as international laws, at www.spamlaws.com. To see the CAN-SPAM Act and proposed legislation for the current Congressional session, go to http://www.spamlaws.com/federal/index.shtml.

For more information about spam, visit the FTC's spam Web site at http://www.ftc.gov/bcp/conline/edcams/spam/index.html. You can also forward spam to spam@uce.gov, which the FTC uses to pursue legal action against spammers. The Web site also includes tips on how to prevent more spam from infesting your inbox.

To read the full Pew Internet & American Life Project report on spam, go to www.pewinternet.org/pdfs/PIP_Data_Memo_on_Spam.pdf.

Abuse.net tracks information about spammers and anti-spam techniques. The page at http://spam.abuse.net/userhelp/ has lots of helpful links to tips and tools on a variety of subjects, including spam filtering and blocking, hiding your e-mail address, sources of disposable e-mail addresses, how to trace a spam message, and how to report spam to a service provider.

Chapter 7

Securing Windows

Millions of computers all over the world use the Windows operating system and Microsoft applications. Many theories exist to explain Microsoft's hegemony: clever marketing; good programmers; the company's willingness to license its software to any PC manufacturer; Apple's insistence on doing the exact opposite, thus ceding significant market share to Microsoft; and monopolistic bullying. Whatever the reasons (and there is a core of truth in each), Microsoft owns the most dominant operating system and application suites on Earth.

This predominance is good for two groups: Microsoft shareholders and the people who create malware. A landscape dominated by a single operating system creates a fertile environment for viruses, worms, Trojan horses, and spyware. All software has vulnerabilities, and all operating systems and application platforms can be exploited. But when one family of software dominates, malware writers who want to have the greatest impact go after that biggest target. The Windows logo could easily be replaced with a bull's-eye.

And when you consider how much the Internet has become an engine of commerce, attacking the most popular software platform is likely to yield the greatest return. Infamous bank robber Willie Sutton was asked, "Why do you rob banks?" His answer was, "Because that's where the money is." The Microsoft code base is the world's biggest bank, so it gets lots of attention from people who try to tunnel in from under the basement, sneak through the roof, break windows, or simply kick in the front door with guns blazing. Criminals are coming at you with a host of schemes, most of which revolve around exploiting the Windows operating system or the Internet Explorer (IE) Web browser.

Is Microsoft really under attack? A test conducted by *USA Today*[1] showed that within a two-week period, 8,177 attempts a day were made to break into a computer running Windows XP Service Pack 1 (SP1) on a DSL Internet connection. That's a startlingly high number, especially considering that the test left out two significant attack vectors: e-mail and Web browsing.

The good news is that only nine of the attempted attacks actually succeeded, and the computer lacked the most recent patches and wasn't using any security software. By contrast, a Windows XP machine running a ZoneAlarm firewall suffered 50 attempts a day, none of which succeeded. (The test also included computers running Mac OS X and Linspire, a consumer-oriented Linux-based operating system from Microtel.) The OS X computer suffered nearly as many attack attempts as the Windows computer running SP1 (although none succeeded). The Linspire machine was attacked fewer than 800 times in total, with no successful intrusions.

The easiest advice I can give you is to consider using a different operating system the next time you buy a computer. Operating system partisans argue that Macintosh and Linux are easier to secure because they are superior products. Whether that's true is beyond my ability to judge. What I can tell you is that the majority of malware is written for the Microsoft platform, and by using an alternative operating system you are less prone to being successfully attacked.

If you are using a Windows computer, it's essential to lock it down. The first thing to do is install a firewall and set it to stealth mode. The next thing to do is ensure that you have all the latest patches for the Windows operating system and all the applications you use (including non-Microsoft applications). Finally, take steps to secure Internet Explorer. You should also consider using an alternative browser, such as Firefox or Opera. While these browsers are not unhackable, they avoid some of the security issues associated with IE and are smaller targets that get far less attention from criminals (although this may change quickly for Firefox as its popularity increases).

---

1. *"Unprotected PCs Can Be Hijacked in Minutes," by Byron Acohido and Jon Swartz,* USA Today, *November 29, 2004.*

This chapter addresses the specifics of securing Windows XP Service Pack 2 (SP2). Windows XP SP2 is the most recent version of the Microsoft operating system for consumers and is the one Microsoft currently supports. We'll also look at how to make IE more secure and where to find alternative browsers.

7.1 Windows XP Service Pack 2

Microsoft is fully aware that its products are under continuous attack. The company is also aware that it risks long-term damage to its reputation (if not to its sales) if Windows continues to be fodder for voracious malware and insidious intruders. Windows XP with Service Pack 2 is part of a concerted effort by Microsoft to improve the security capabilities of the Windows platform and to reverse its reputation as worm bait. The SP2 upgrade is available for free, assuming you've already purchased XP. If you're using an older version of Windows, you'll have to purchase a new operating system, which should come with SP2 included.

If you're already running Windows XP, you can download SP2 from Windows Update (but it's a large file, so be sure to set aside some time for download), or you can order the upgrade on a CD-ROM at www.microsoft.com/windowsxp/sp2/default.mspx. Registered Windows XP users can get the CD delivered for free.

The following section looks at what's new in SP2—in particular, the protection mechanisms built into the software.

Windows Security Center

The major improvement in SP2 is the Security Center, which places several important security controls in one location. From the Security Center you can monitor the status of anti-virus (AV) software, manage the Windows Firewall, and set up automatic software updates.

To access the Security Center, click the Start button and then choose Control Panel and Security Center (it's the shield icon). When the Security Center window opens, you see three main panels: Firewall, Automatic Updates, and Virus Protection (see Figure 7.1). Each panel has a status light to indicate whether the associated function is on. Each includes a button that actives a small pull-down screen that includes more information about each function.

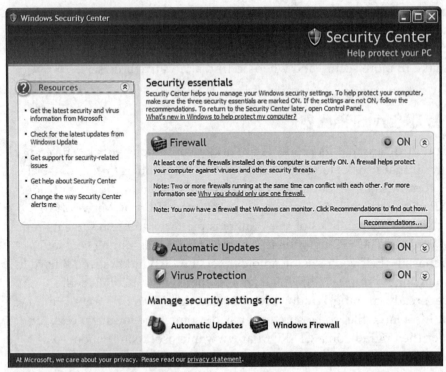

Figure 7.1 The Windows Security Center.

Under the panels are two icons: Automatic Updates, and Windows Firewall. You can click each icon to activate functions and change settings. A Resources window in the upper-left corner provides links to additional security information.

Let's start with the Windows Firewall icon. Windows XP SP2 includes a basic firewall that prevents other machines on the Internet from connecting to your computer unless you connect to them first. The Windows Firewall is turned on by default, so if you are using this as your only firewall, it's already activated.

As discussed in Chapter 3, "Firewalls," while the Windows Firewall is excellent for blocking unsolicited connections that come from the Internet to your computer, it won't do anything about a worm or virus that gets on your machine and tries to initiate connections from your computer to the Internet. Thus, the Windows Firewall does only half the job (although the more important half). A proper firewall should also monitor your computer's attempts to initiate connections with the Internet. That's because malware and spyware often open Internet connections to report back to a control server, get updated instructions, or launch attacks against new targets. Thus, a firewall that monitors outbound communications can alert you if a suspicious program suddenly wants to talk to someone on the Internet.

Chapter 3 lists numerous firewalls that offer both functions, and we recommend that you get one of these and install it on your computer. If you do use a different firewall, you need to disable the Windows Firewall first. You won't be doubly protected by using a third-party firewall at the same time as the Windows Firewall. In fact, running two or more firewalls on the same machine simultaneously may disrupt your Internet usage. To disable the Windows Firewall, click the Windows Firewall icon at the bottom of the Security Center page. A pop-up window opens, as shown in Figure 7.2; simply click the Off button. Some third-party firewalls can also turn off the Windows Firewall during installation.

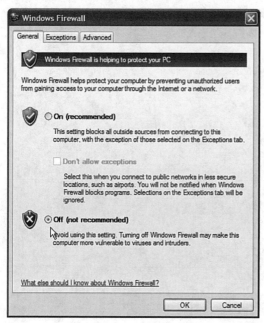

Figure 7.2   The Windows Firewall page.

Even if you turn off the Windows Firewall, the Security Center can still let you know if it finds a third-party firewall and whether that firewall is on. Microsoft should be able to find most of the well-known firewalls.

Configuring the Windows Firewall

If you do run the Windows Firewall, you shouldn't have to bother with a lot of configuration issues for general tasks like Web surfing and sending and receiving e-mail. However, you need to be aware of some basic configuration issues. The firewall may prevent some programs, such as games or instant-messaging software, from opening a connection to the Internet. You can change that by clicking the Windows Firewall icon at the bottom of the Security Center page. The window shown in Figure 7.2 appears. Click the Exceptions tab. You see a list titled Programs and Services," as shown in Figure 7.3. Search this list to see if the program you want to allow to communicate with the Internet is there. If it isn't, click the Add Program button and then search the Programs list, as shown in Figure 7.4. Select the program and click OK. This moves the program to the Programs and Services list, as shown in Figure 7.3. Make sure the program you added is checked, and then click the OK button. Windows Firewall then will allow that program to access the Internet.

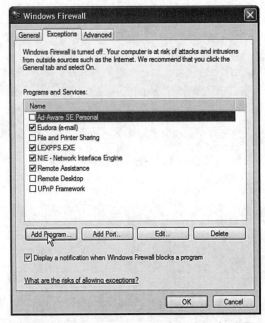

Figure 7.3 The Exceptions tab of the Windows Firewall.

Figure 7.4   The Add a Program dialog box.

You should keep the number of exceptions as small as possible. The more exceptions you create, the more holes you poke in the firewall, which increases the chance that an intruder or piece of malware will be able to access your computer.

You can also add ports to the exceptions list. A port is an opening to your computer that allows a specific program or service to communicate with your computer. For instance, Web traffic uses port 80. Your computer knows which ports need to be open for common applications like the Internet and e-mail. Some programs use a variety of ports (online games, VoIP telephony, and instant messaging are good examples), so you may need to manually open those ports to allow the program to work. As with programs, however, the fewer ports you open, the fewer holes there are in your firewall.

If you know the port (or ports) you want to open, click the Add Port... button on the screen shown in Figure 7.3. This opens a new window called Add a Port, as shown in Figure 7.5. It allows you to enter the port name and number.

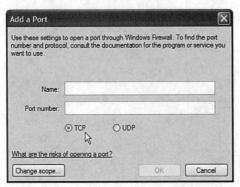

Figure 7.5 The Add a Port dialog box.

You can also use the Advanced tab to further configure the firewall, as shown in Figure 7.6. This window includes four sections: Network Connection Settings, Security Logging, ICMP, and Default Settings.

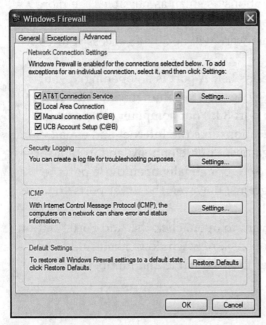

Figure 7.6 The Advanced tab of the Windows Firewall.

Under Network Connection Settings you should see the connection to your service provider.

Under Security Logging you can create a security log to see the connections that have been allowed and denied. These logs make little sense unless you have some experience with computer networking, but if you're interested in seeing what an IP address looks like, what ports your computer is using, and the IP addresses of the places you connect to, you should take a look at the log. (You can see a sample log in Figure 3.2 in Chapter 3.) Windows XP SP2 has a default file destination for the logs (C:WINDOWS/pfirewall), but you can have the file written anywhere you like. Note that this log function works only for the Windows Firewall. If you're using a third-party firewall product, it creates its own logs, which you should be able to find through the user interface.

The log format includes the date and time of each action, a description of the action (for example, to open a connection to another computer), the protocol (TCP and so on), the source and destination IP addresses, the source (that's you) and destination ports, and information about the individual packets that make up Internet communications. For more information about ports, protocols, and Internet communications, see Chapter 3.

The ICMP section of the Advanced tab enables the computer to send and receive Internet Control Message Protocol (ICMP) messages. ICMP is useful for administrators of computer networks to get information about the system's health, but there's little need for home computer users to bother with ICMP messages. In fact, some attackers use ICMP messages to see if a computer will respond. Thus, your best bet is not to enable any ICMP messages.

Finally, the Default Settings section is your starting-over point if all this meddling is causing problems with your Internet experience. Simply click Restore Defaults to set the Windows Firewall to its original settings. Note that clicking the Restore Defaults button wipes out any changes you've made to the firewall, including programs you've allowed, ports you've opened, and so on.

Virus Protection

Windows XP SP2 does not offer native virus protection, but it can inform you if a third-party AV program is present and whether that program has all the latest virus updates. However, note that Microsoft does not monitor all AV software programs. You can find out if your AV software is supported by surfing to www.microsoft.com/security/partners/antivirus.asp. A partial list of supported AV programs includes Symantec, Trend Micro, Computer Associates, GFI, F-Secure, Sophos, Kaspersky, McAfee, and Panda Software.

Note that while Microsoft doesn't offer consumer anti-virus software (although this is likely to change, possibly with the release of a new Microsoft operating system), it does have a free utility to check your computer for common malware. The Malicious Software Removal Tool scans your computer for a list of malicious software and then removes any malware it finds. As I was writing this chapter, the tool detected 20 families (including variants) of known worms and viruses. If you are running third-party anti-virus software, you should already be protected from these malware families. However, if you're curious, it doesn't hurt to download the tool and see what it finds. You can download the tool at www.microsoft.com/security/malwareremove.

If you have turned on Automatic Updates (see the section "Turning on Automatic Updates"), the tool is automatically downloaded and run for you. When the tool finishes running, it deletes itself. Keep in mind that this tool is not a substitute for a dedicated anti-virus program. Even though it can remove common forms of malware, it does not prevent that malware from getting onto your computer in the first place. By contrast, an up-to-date anti-virus product can detect and block malware before it can install itself on your computer. In addition, the Malicious Software Removal Tool detects and removes only a small subset of the malware that can be detected and removed by a dedicated anti-virus product.

Buffer Overflow Protection

SP2 helps protect the Windows operating system and several communications protocols from an attack technique known as buffer overflow. Using this technique, a malicious program attempts to inject more code into an area of the computer's memory (called the buffer) than the computer can handle. The excess code, which usually contains instructions for taking control of the computer, flows into another area of memory and gets executed. Automated worms rely almost exclusively on buffer overflows. Most computer operating systems and applications are vulnerable to buffer overflows. SP2 doesn't eliminate the threat of buffer overflows, but it does improve Windows' resistance.

7.2 Patch Tuesday

All software is a perpetual work in progress; there is never a point in time in which software is finished. Sometimes that's because the software vendors release the next version of the software, which boasts new features and functionalities.

However, between specific releases, software vendors also release patches. These patches are chunks of software that correct problems in the program. Some of these problems are functional bugs that interfere with the program's normal operation. For instance, a software bug might make your onscreen calculator say that 2+2 equals 5.

There also exists a special category of bug called vulnerabilities. A vulnerability is a flaw or weakness in a software program that can be exploited by someone other than the computer's owner to get the computer to do something the exploiter wants. Many worms that sweep through the Internet are examples of malware that are designed to exploit software vulnerabilities. Sometimes the vulnerabilities are discovered by the organization that created the software. What's more likely is that a researcher outside the organization finds it. Many companies make a business out of finding software vulnerabilities. Three of the best-known are Secunia, eEye, and X-Force (which is the research arm of a security company called Internet Security Systems). These research organizations gain publicity for their prowess in uncovering vulnerabilities, and so, like newspapers try to scoop one another, these researchers are constantly trying to one-up their competitors.

When a legitimate research organization discovers a software vulnerability, the accepted protocol is to contact the vendor of the affected software. Usually the research organization agrees to give the vendor a time frame (say, 30 days, but the time varies considerably) in which to confirm that the vulnerability exists and to create a patch. When the patch is ready, the researcher and the organization publicly announce the vulnerability so that consumers and businesses can download the fix.

Unfortunately, not everyone feels bound by such a protocol. Shadowy researchers may discover vulnerabilities and not notify the affected software vendor. They can keep these vulnerabilities to themselves to exploit, or share or sell the information to others. In some cases they announce the vulnerability publicly so that the vendor and the attacker community find out about it at the same time. In that case, the race is on as the vendor scrambles to create a fix and the attacker community scrambles to create an exploit.

To make matters worse, exploit writers are releasing attack tools at an ever-quickening pace. For example, in October 2000 Microsoft announced a patch for a vulnerability in its server software. Almost a year later the Nimda worm appeared, which attacked the vulnerability. By contrast, in April 2004 Microsoft announced another patch for its server software; 17 days later the Sasser worm leapt onto the scene.

The other problem with patches is that people don't install them even when they are available. Although a patch had been available for 336 days before the Nimda worm emerged, enough people hadn't installed the patch that Nimda found all the vulnerable machines it needed to effect a widespread outbreak.

Microsoft used to announce patches at random. But as the number of vulnerabilities has increased, the company decided to set up a regular patch schedule. Now Microsoft announces the latest round of software updates on the second Tuesday of every month. Microsoft also highlights patches that address critical vulnerabilities. Critical vulnerabilities are usually those that could give a remote attacker control over the machine or otherwise cause grievous harm. Patch Tuesdays usually include at least one critical vulnerability per batch. Of course, Microsoft also issues emergency patches outside the scheduled release if the vulnerability is particularly dangerous.

Windows XP SP2 includes capabilities for automatic updating. You can configure your computer to go to Microsoft's Web site on a regular basis to check for new patches. Home users are strongly encouraged to turn on Automatic Updates because, as mentioned, attackers can release attack tools within days or weeks of an announced vulnerability. By automatically updating your system, you enjoy immediate protection against forthcoming attacks. Another benefit is that you don't have to remember to visit Microsoft every month for the latest and greatest fixes. Finally, the automatic service is convenient, because it addresses patches for a broad range of Microsoft products, including the Windows operating system, Internet Explorer, and popular applications. Thus, if a new vulnerability is uncovered in Windows Media Player, for example, you don't need to go to a separate site to get the patch.

Turning on Automatic Updates

To turn on Automatic Updates, click the Automatic Updates icon at the bottom of the Security Center screen, as shown in Figure 7.1. This opens a smaller window called Automatic Updates, which allows you to choose your settings (see Figure 7.7).

You can choose to have updates downloaded and installed automatically (which is Microsoft's recommended setting), or you can choose the frequency and time at which the updates happen. If you choose a time when your computer is usually off, the updates are installed the next time you restart your computer. Just to be safe, I recommend choosing a time when you're usually online to ensure that the updates get delivered.

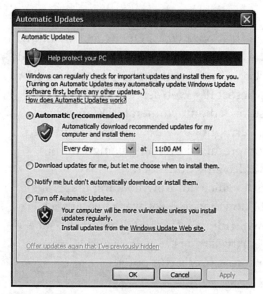

Figure 7.7   The Automatic Updates dialog box.

You can also choose to have the updates downloaded automatically but installed only at your request, or you can choose to be notified that updates are available without downloading or installing them automatically. You can also turn off Automatic Updates.

You can also check to ensure that you have all the updates you need by going to http://windowsupdate.microsoft.com. (You have to use Internet Explorer version 5 or higher to access this site—it won't work with Firefox.) Once you arrive at the site, Microsoft gives you two choices: Express Install, which downloads only critical and security updates, and Custom Install, which lets you select specific updates from a list.

7.3 Securing Internet Explorer

Just as Windows is the most widely deployed operating system in the world, Internet Explorer is the most widely used Internet browser. This situation presents a familiar problem: Bad guys improve their chances of taking control of your computer or installing software without your permission by attacking the most widely used browser.

Internet Explorer Security

Attackers can manipulate Internet Explorer in several ways. One way is by taking advantage of software vulnerabilities in the application. For instance, in June 2004 a Trojan horse called Download.ject emerged. This attack exploited software flaws in both Internet Information Server (IIS, Microsoft's Web server platform) and Internet Explorer. Malicious code was first loaded onto vulnerable Web servers. Then a Trojan horse keystroke logger was surreptitiously downloaded onto the computers of visitors who surfed to the compromised Web site using Internet Explorer. Download.ject is an example of a drive-by download.

Another tactic is to use the browser as a vehicle for downloading malicious code. Attackers can either trick a user into downloading software (using social engineering) or force the browser into downloading software without the user's knowledge by taking advantage of low security settings. Spyware and adware often rely on the Web browser to gain entry to a user's computer.

Dealing with ActiveX

One of the reasons that Web browsing is a popular spyware and malware vehicle is ActiveX. ActiveX is a Microsoft technology that makes Web pages more interactive—for example, through animation or through the ability to open other applications in a browser (such as Microsoft Word or Adobe). Besides enlivening Web pages, ActiveX technology can also execute programs, called ActiveX controls, on your computer via Internet Explorer. ActiveX controls interact with the operating system just like any other executable software. Some ActiveX controls are harmless and improve your browsing experience, but malware writers can also create ActiveX controls to install unwanted programs on your computer.

ActiveX checks the digital signature associated with a piece of software to be downloaded. A digital signature ensures that the creators of the software are who they claim to be. While a digital signature doesn't ensure that the actual program is safe, it can help you spot programs that are trying to masquerade as a different kind of software. It's recommended that you not accept any software with an invalid digital signature.

You can adjust the settings of the IE browser so that it opens a window to warn you when an ActiveX control wants to be downloaded and gives you the choice to install or not install the download (see Figure 7.8).

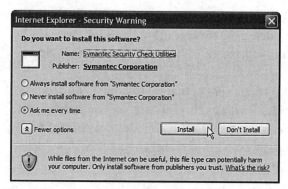

Figure 7.8 Internet Explorer security warning.

To check the setting, open IE and choose Tools and then Internet Options. This opens the Internet Options window.

Click the Security tab, as shown in Figure 7.9. You see four Web zones for which you can adjust security settings: Internet, Local intranet, Trusted sites, and Restricted sites. Each zone has its own security settings that it applies to any Web sites you add to the zones. Any Web site not explicitly listed in a zone gets the security settings of the Internet zone. (You don't need to do anything with the Local intranet setting, which is for Windows PCs that are part of a corporate network.)

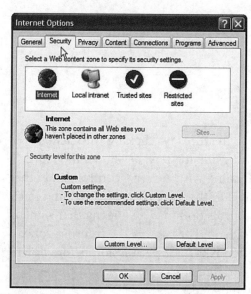

Figure 7.9 The Security tab of the Internet Options dialog box.

To add Web sites to the Trusted Sites and Restricted sites zones, simply click the zone you want to adjust and then click the Sites... button. In the new dialog box that opens, simply type in the Web address of each site you want to include in each zone.

You can then change the security settings for each zone to adjust the security instructions and configurations associated with each Web site you've included in the zone. To change the settings for each zone, click the zone icon you want to adjust. You should see a slider bar that allows you to change the settings, which range from Low to High (see Figure 7.10).

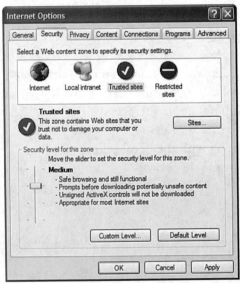

Figure 7.10   Adjusting the settings for Trusted Sites.

You can also play with individual security features by clicking the Custom Level... button. This opens the Security Settings dialog box, as shown in Figure 7.11. Here you can set individual rules for dealing with ActiveX controls and other browser functions. For instance, for Web sites in the Trusted zone, you can select Enable for the Download signed ActiveX controls option. This means that signed ActiveX controls download without notifying you. For sites in the Internet zone, you can choose Prompt so that your computer asks your permission before downloading signed ActiveX controls. For the Restricted sites zone, you can choose Disable so that no ActiveX control gets downloaded.

Figure 7.11 Customizing the security settings.

Be aware that tweaking individual settings inside the Security Settings window may affect your browsing experience. You can also choose one of the options (High, Medium, Medium-Low, or Low) in the Reset custom settings area if you don't want to play around with individual settings. If you have played around with settings and have gotten hopelessly muddled, you can click the Reset button as shown in Figure 7.11. This will reset your changes to the Microsoft default settings.

Note that as long as you've set the IE Security setting to Medium you get a warning message; any other setting below that allows ActiveX controls to download without notification. It is recommended that you choose the Medium setting at least for the Trusted zone. For the Internet zone, I would choose the High setting first and see if it disrupts your browsing experience. Remember, you can always put trusted sites into the Trusted zone with a lower setting. However, I wouldn't go any lower than Medium for the Internet zone. Obviously, you should choose the High setting for sites in the Restricted zone (or just don't visit sites that you would put into a Restricted zone in the first place).

Windows XP SP2 adds a toolbar (called the Information Bar) to Internet Explorer that appears when a signed ActiveX control needs to be downloaded (see Figure 7.12). The Information Bar appears under any other toolbars you've added to Internet Explorer. When you click the Information Bar, it gives you the option to download the ActiveX control or get more information about the potential risks of accepting the download.

Figure 7.12   The Information Bar.

If you accept the download, a dialog box appears to confirm that you want to install the software. If the software is properly signed, the dialog box shows you the name of the software and the software's publisher and provides Web links to give you more information about the software and its publisher (see Figure 7.8).

Unfortunately, even if a dialog box pops up to alert you of an unsigned ActiveX control, clicking No doesn't always help. Some malware writers manipulate the dialog box so that clicking No or any other button still downloads the software. Attackers may also try to disguise these pop-up messages to look like messages from Windows or make them appear to be generated by the Web site you're visiting. These messages are usually alarmist and prompt you to take some action immediately, such as clicking the Yes button to run a scan or download a program to repair the "problem." You should ignore these messages.

To close dialog boxes and pop-ups without clicking the No or Cancel button or the X in the upper-right corner, you can press Alt-F4. This safely closes windows inside a browser without allowing any downloads.

Privacy Configuration

The Internet Options window has other options besides the Security tab to make changes to Internet Explorer, including General (where you can set your home page, store temporary Internet files, and configure the record of pages you've visited) and Privacy. This section looks in more detail at the Privacy settings.

The Privacy settings let you control how cookies are stored on your computer (see Figure 7.13). A cookie is a small file that Web sites store on your computer hard drive to customize your browsing experience. For instance, cookies help e-commerce sites remember their users' preferences. Cookies should be covered in a Web site's privacy policy. The privacy policy outlines how a Web site collects and shares information about its users. In general, cookies are relatively harmless.

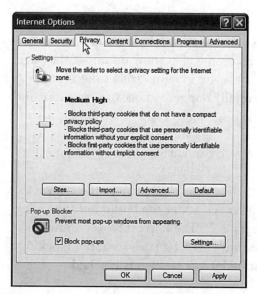

Figure 7.13 Adjusting cookie settings in IE.

However, some cookies track you as you surf the Web to see what other sites you visit, sometimes with personally identifiable information, such as your name or address. This information is used as "market research" to help provide more targeted advertising. Other cookies are loaded onto your hard drive and aren't covered by any privacy policy.

The Privacy setting includes a slider bar that configures how your browser deals with cookies. Settings range from accepting all cookies to blocking all cookies. By sliding the bar up and down, you can see how each setting deals with cookies deposited by the site you're visiting and with third-party cookies. Microsoft defines third-party cookies as those that don't originate from the same domain as the Web site you are visiting. Third-party cookies are most likely tracking cookies. My suggestion is to use the High or Medium-High setting.

You can also create policies for specific Web sites. Click the Sites... button to add sites to a list that always accepts or always blocks cookies. You can also override the settings from the slider bar by clicking the Advanced... button.

Note that Web sites rely heavily on cookies to make browsing easier. If you choose to block all cookies or to be prompted to accept cookies, you will spend a lot of time clicking Accept or Deny as you visit Web pages.

Pop-Up Blocker

Many Web sites generate pop-up ads as you visit the site. Pop-up ads open new windows in front of the page you're viewing. (Some also show up under the page; you see them after you close the browser. These are imaginatively called "pop-unders.") These ads are annoying and potentially dangerous because spyware and adware use pop-up windows as a way of tricking you to install their programs.

Windows SP2 running Internet Explorer 6.0 lets you suppress these ads with Pop-Up Blocker. It is enabled by default, but you can customize it or turn it off if you choose.

To turn on (or turn off) Pop-Up Blocker, click the Privacy tab in the Internet Options window. You see the Block pop-ups checkbox at the bottom of the dialog box (see Figure 7.13). To configure, click Settings.... The Pop-up Blocker Settings dialog box, shown in Figure 7.14, lets you exempt specific sites from the blocking function. You can also select how to be notified if a pop-up gets blocked.

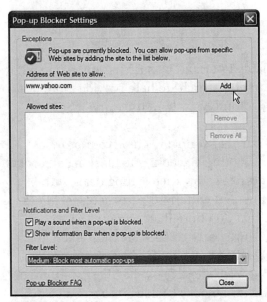

Figure 7.14   The Pop-up Blocker Settings dialog box.

Next, you can set the filter level to Low, Medium, or High. Low allows pop-ups from secure sites (that is, sites using HTTPS, such as your bank's Web site). Medium blocks most pop-ups, except those that come from Web sites you have listed in the Trusted zone. The High setting should block all pop-ups. I recommend the Medium or High setting.

You can also download free tools that block pop-ups. For instance, both Yahoo! and Google offer browser toolbars that can block pop-ups. Go to http://toolbar.yahoo.com or http://toolbar.google.com. Toolbars are available for other browsers as well.

7.4 Browser Alternatives

The best way to prevent the most common attacks is to stay away from the most prominent targets. As mentioned, all software has flaws and can be attacked, but Microsoft's Internet Explorer browser is clearly the target of choice for attackers. Alternative Web browsers such as Firefox and Opera are distant seconds in the race against Microsoft. Thus, the great advantage of these browsers is that they attract less attention from Internet criminals. They have essential elements such as pop-up blocking, and they also have cooler features than Internet Explorer, like tabbed browsing, which lets you open multiple windows in a single browser.

Aside from low market penetration, another reason these browsers are more secure is that they don't use ActiveX. Rather, they use a technology called Java applets. Like ActiveX, Java applets can enhance the browsing experience and help with software downloads. Unlike ActiveX, Java applets are not integrated with the computer's operating system, which makes it harder for malware to gain a foothold. Java applets are also run inside what is called a sandbox. The sandbox isolates the applet and gives it access to only limited computing resources inside the sandbox. It's possible to exploit and misuse Java applets, but overall they provide a higher level of protection.

That said, these browsers are not magic protection against attackers. If you do choose an alternative, the security mantra of "keep the software updated" certainly applies. You have to stay on top of security fixes and newly discovered vulnerabilities on your own—the automatic Windows Update system does not work for non-Microsoft products.

Ironically, as these alternatives get more popular (many millions of people have already downloaded the Firefox browser), they naturally will attract more attention from criminals. More vulnerabilities will be uncovered, more exploits will target the browser, and it will give up the security advantage that comes with being the underdog (or underfox?).

Another downside is that many Web sites have been optimized for Internet Explorer, which means that an alternative browser may have trouble fully rendering a Web site and all its functions. For example, I was unable to use Firefox to order a book at Amazon; I had to switch back to IE to get the transaction to work. However, there's no rule against having multiple browsers on your computer. Many people use an alternative browser for general Web surfing and fire up IE only when necessary.

The next sections look at Firefox and Opera, two of the most popular alternatives to Internet Explorer.

Firefox (www.mozilla.org)

The most popular of the alternative browsers is Firefox, available as a free download. Firefox is based on open-source software; that means anyone who wants it can get a copy of the source code. The source code is the most essential set of software instructions that tell the application or program how to work. Users are welcome to tinker with the source code to find bugs, suggest improvements, and add new features and functions that are then made available to the rest of the community of users. Most open-source software is available for free and is maintained by volunteers.

The opposite of open-source software is proprietary software. The source code of proprietary software is jealously guarded by the company that owns it. New features, functions, and bug fixes are created and released by the company, on the company's own schedule.

One of the benefits of open-source software is that because so many different people can work on it at once, it tends to engender lots of interesting or fun add-ons. You can see these add-ons (which Mozilla calls extensions) at https://addons.mozilla.org/.

As mentioned, Firefox is not free of problems. It is still subject to vulnerabilities and potential exploits, and you have to stay abreast of them. To see the current list of vulnerabilities in the browser, check out www.mozilla.org/projects/security/known-vulnerabilities.html. This page lists vulnerabilities that have been addressed with each new release of the Firefox software. It also assigns a criticality rating to each vulnerability.

To find the most recent version of Firefox, including security fixes, go to www.mozilla.org/security/. If you already use Firefox and you want to check for the latest upgrade, select Tools and then Options, which opens a dialog box. In the dialog box click Advanced. You see the dialog box shown in Figure 7.15. Scroll down the screen until you come to the Software Update entry. If you check the Periodically check for updates to: boxes, the Firefox browser will check the Firefox Web site every day for new updates. Note that Firefox does not automatically install these updates—it prompts you before installing any software. When you click Check Now, Firefox automatically checks for new versions of the software.

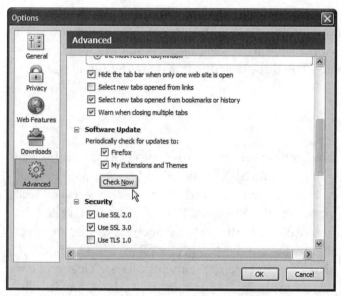

Figure 7.15   Checking for Firefox software updates.

Opera (www.opera.com)

Opera is available in two versions: one is free, and the other costs $39. The free version generates advertising. When you install the free version of Opera, you can choose between receiving targeted ads from Google or generic ads. If you select targeted Google ads, your computer's IP address and the URLs you visit are sent to Google to help generate ads that match your browsing preferences. Google also tries to determine your geographic location based on your IP address to help target advertising. Opera says it does not collect personally identifiable information about you. You can find more information at www.opera.com/adsupport/ and at www.opera.com/privacy.

I tried the generic ad version. The browser dedicates a small area in the top-right corner of the page to banner ads; it's not very intrusive and certainly tolerable. If you really like the Opera browser but can't stand the advertising, you can license a copy for $39, and all the ads will go away.

7.5 Security Checks

It's one thing to set up a firewall and twiddle with Internet Explorer controls, but even better is to check your work. The Internet is full of resources for checking your computer's security status. The three described next are definitely worth investigating.

ShieldsUP! (www.grc.com)

ShieldsUP! is a free service for checking the security settings of personal firewalls, including the Windows Firewall built into SP2. As noted in Chapter 3, ShieldsUP! has been run by security guru Steve Gibson for years. The site offers several tests, including two that are appropriate for the Windows Firewall. The first, called Common Ports, checks 26 often-used ports that may be open (and thus are accessible to bad guys). The second test, Service Ports, checks 1,056. It's a more comprehensive test and takes a bit longer. In either case the results are clear and easy to understand and can give you a sense of whether your firewall is doing its job. The site also includes links to more information about personal firewalls and computer security.

To run the tests, go to www.grc.com and scroll down to the ShieldsUP! link. By using the service you are granting formal permission for the ShieldsUP! utility to scan your computer. ShieldsUP! tells you the IP address of the computer used to scan your machine, so if you're curious, you can go back and look at the firewall logs after you run the scan to see what the scan looked like from your firewall's perspective.

PivX PreView (www.pivx.com/preview)

PreView is a free security tool from a company called PivX. The tool gives your computer a security grade based on four categories: Threat Center, Security

Software, Patches/HotFixes, and Firewall Protection. PreView analyzes your computer to calculate a security score using these four categories. It's a simple way to communicate how vulnerable your computer is to attack. However, a significant portion of your score is based on whether you've purchased another PivX product, so take the score with a grain of salt.

Symantec Security Check (www.symantec.com/securitycheck/)

Symantec Security Check scans your computer for a variety of potential vulnerabilities, including ports that may respond to unsolicited requests, the presence of Trojan horses, and whether you are running anti-virus software. The test results are understandable, and detailed results are available for the Hacker Test (which shows the ports that do or don't respond to connection requests). The check requires an ActiveX download to operate.

7.6 Internet Explorer 7.0 and Windows Vista

Microsoft is planning significant upgrades to Internet Explorer and the Windows operating system. Internet Explorer 7.0 will probably be available in the fall of 2005. Although details were sketchy as this chapter was being written, Microsoft has promised that IE 7.0 will include beefed-up security and new tools to enhance the browsing experience. Many observers had expected Microsoft to hold off on releasing a new version of IE until after the company released its new operating system. However, Microsoft bumped up the release date after witnessing the incredible surge of Firefox and other alternative browsers. (That said, Internet Explorer still counts for approximately 90 percent of all browsers in use, so Firefox has a way to go yet.)

Windows Vista (formerly code-named Longhorn), the new operating system, is expected to arrive in late Fall 2006. Again, details are scarce, but Microsoft has promised new security enhancements as well as slicker graphics, a new file storage system, and the ability to run Internet Explorer in a containment area to make it harder for malware to use the browser as an entry point onto your computer.

7.7 Checklist

Use this checklist as a quick-reference guide to the material covered in this chapter.

Do

- Turn on Automatic Updates to ensure that your Microsoft software has the latest software fixes and security patches.
- Take advantage of the security capabilities in Windows Security Center, including firewall and anti-virus monitoring.
- Use the Windows Firewall if you don't have a third-party firewall.
- Consider using an alternative Web browser for surfing the Internet.
- Take steps to ensure that Internet Explorer prompts you before installing ActiveX controls.

Don't

- Forget to keep Windows and Internet Explorer updated.
- Accept unsigned ActiveX controls.
- Forget to keep alternative browsers updated with the latest software fixes.
- Run two or more firewalls on the same machine simultaneously.

7.8 Helpful Resources

This section presents additional resources to help you learn more.

Microsoft has a variety of security information for consumers and is a good place to start for understanding some security basics. Go to www.microsoft.com/athome/security to learn more about securing Windows and Microsoft applications.

CastleCops is a user forum for a variety of topics about computers, including security. You can join a forum to ask questions, read posts, and get helpful information about almost everything under the sun related to computers. In particular, if you surf to http://castlecops.com/forums, you can scroll down the list to find forums about browsers (including browser security) and operating systems (including Windows and Windows security).

Security research organization Secunia tracks patched and unpatched security flaws in Windows and several popular browsers, including Internet Explorer and Firefox. The write-ups are technical in nature, but the site is a great clearinghouse to check up on the latest vulnerabilities that may be affecting your computer. Go to www.secunia.com.

Chapter 8

Keeping Your Family Safe Online

The Internet presents a significant challenge for conscientious parents. Whether you are trying to screen out objectionable material such as pornography and violence or thwart the child predators who stalk chat rooms, the Internet opens an endless number of avenues to Web sites and Web denizens you don't want in your home. On the other hand, parents might need protecting from their children. The music and movie industries take copyright violations very seriously these days, and you may find yourself entangled in lawsuits or assessed with hefty fines because your kid downloaded *Star Wars: Episode III—Revenge of the Sith* or a hit song without giving the copyright holders their cut.

In the corporate world, several companies have turned Web filtering into a highly profitable business. Their products contain huge lists of sites that a company might not want its employees looking at for liability reasons (pornography in the workplace can constitute a hostile environment and result in lawsuits) or productivity reasons (sports, gambling, and e-commerce sites tend to distract employees from the tasks at hand). Corporations also invest in technologies to detect and block the peer-to-peer file-sharing programs that enable copyright violations.

Similar technical solutions are available for the home (although they aren't as extensive and certainly aren't foolproof), but parents can benefit from nontechnical tools as well, including common sense and the time-honored parental skill of vigilance.

This chapter looks at solutions to screening out unwanted material from the Web. We'll discuss the potential legal and financial ramifications of file sharing and look at some of the security issues associated with peer-to-peer software. We will also discuss online safety issues, such as protecting your kids from online predators. Some of the problems discussed here have technological solutions, or at least there are tools to help you solve them. But in most cases the best defense is to instill good Internet common sense in your children. Remember that the Internet is just like any other community—it's got its safe areas and dangerous places, and the standard advice about not talking to strangers applies.

8.1 Filtering Unwanted Content

When I was a kid there were only three avenues to illicit material: finding the racy parts in the popular novels my parents had around the house; stumbling across discarded girlie magazines; and wading doggedly through hours of R-rated movies during sleepovers at the house of a friend who had cable, hoping for a glimpse of the female form.

These days the situation is dramatically different. The Internet is the world's largest repository of filth, and it's all just a few search queries away. This shouldn't come as a surprise. Pornography has migrated to practically every mass medium that humans have devised, including photography, print, film, cable television, and home video. About the only medium that doesn't draw significant revenues from pornography is radio (although Howard Stern seems to be giving it a shot). I don't know when the first naked picture was transmitted from one computer to another across a telephone line, but I'd bet that it was within the first week that the computers were hooked up.

And pornography is only one head on the objectionable-content Hydra: There's also violence, hate sites, gambling, chat rooms, and so on. Compounding the problem is that the Internet lacks many of the filters that are present in other mediums. A bookstore won't sell *Playboy* to an 11-year-old, but a Web browser will dutifully serve up objectionable content by the ton.

Parents have a variety of technical and nontechnical options at hand. We'll suggest a few ideas for monitoring your kids' online activity and explain how to use search engine and Web browser filters. However, because of the incredible number of options for delivering content, the most robust solution (aside from disconnecting the Internet) is likely to require third-party monitoring software.

Human Monitoring

The coarsest filter is to simply not let your kids have Internet access in a private area, like their bedrooms. If you designate a computer in a common area like the living room as the one the kids use for online activities, you exercise some influence over the kinds of things they do online. Knowing that anyone else passing by can catch a glance at the screen should limit the objectionable content they might otherwise seek. This may be difficult in a household where more than one person needs Internet access simultaneously, or if you've installed a wireless access point that reaches throughout the house, but a good family rule of "If you're on the Internet, you are in the living room or at the kitchen table" or some such variant may help.

You can also check up on what your kids are doing online by viewing the History records in the Web browser. Every Web browser provides an area where you can see each page visited over a specific period of time, such as a week or a month. You can click the sites listed and visit the actual Web pages, and some browsers let you search the History records for specific sites. The History function is useful for tracking down sites you want to revisit but for which you can't remember the exact address. It's also useful for monitoring your kids' Internet activity.

To check the History in Internet Explorer (IE), as shown in Figure 8.1, choose View, Explorer Bar, History. Inside the History record you can click View to get different options for viewing the record: by date, by site, by most visited, and by order visited.

To set the number of days that pages will be remembered, select Tools, Internet Options. A small window appears that has several tabs across the top. Choose the General tab, which displays a small box for configuring the History settings (see Figure 8.2). You can store site records from 0 to 999 days, but a couple of weeks or a month should be sufficient.

Figure 8.1   Viewing the history in Internet Explorer.

Figure 8.2   Setting the number of days that pages will be remembered.

If you're using Firefox, you can view the page history by clicking View, Sidebar, History. A window appears that runs along the left side of the browser. As in Internet Explorer, you can use the View button to look at the History by date, site, most visited, and last visited. You can set the duration of the History record by selecting Tools, Options. In the Options window, click the Privacy icon. This opens an inner window that includes the History configuration field.

The free version of the Opera browser has very simple access to the records of sites visited, including an icon marked History in a pane on the left side of the browser. You can also select Tools, History. To control how long sites are stored, select Tools, Preferences. When the Preferences window opens, click History near the bottom of the list on the left side of the window. Unlike IE and Firefox, Opera doesn't store sites by date. Instead, you can select how many sites it will store, from 0 to 10,000; once the site limit is reached, old sites drop off as new ones get added.

You might have noticed that each browser also includes a Clear History button, as shown in Figure 8.2. Clicking this button erases the current History records. While this prevents you from seeing what sites your kids may have visited, this also indicates that they may have been visiting sites that they don't want you to know about. Thus, one family rule you may want to establish is that no one is to click the Clear History button.

Don't feel compelled to be sneaky about monitoring online activity; you're not trying to run a sting operation. In fact, if you tell your kids that you are checking up on their Internet activity, you may help reign in their more mischievous impulses.

Search Engine Filtering

Popular search engines can be set to filter explicit sexual content from both keyword and image searches. Search engine filtering doesn't require additional software and is easy to configure. However, these search engines don't guarantee that unwanted material won't appear in search results. It's also easy to switch the filters on and off. In addition, you have to save these preferences in each search engine and in each Web browser you use. For example, if you set Strict filtering for Google using Internet Explorer, that setting won't be applied to Google when you use Firefox until you configure it manually. Finally, trying to configure every possible search engine available on the Internet is futile.

So is there any reason to bother? Yes. Configuring the filters on major search engines adds an extra layer of protection and communicates to everyone using the Web that explicit material isn't allowed. Second, it may help keep younger children (who aren't trying to get around parental restriction) from inadvertently viewing explicit content.

- Google filtering has three settings: Strict filtering, which removes explicit sexual content from image and keyword searches; Moderate, which filters explicit images only (this is the default setting); and No Filtering, which opens the floodgates. To choose a setting, click the Preferences link on the Google home page, as shown in Figure 8.3. This opens a page that lets you adjust particular settings, including a section called SafeSearch. Simply scroll down to the SafeSearch Filtering area and select one of the settings, as shown in Figure 8.4. You can then save your preferences, but these preferences can be changed by anyone who uses the browser.

Figure 8.3   The Preferences link on the Google home page.

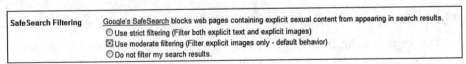

Figure 8.4   Google's SafeSearch area.

- Yahoo! offers SafeSearch filtering with three settings: filtering explicit content from Web, image, and video searches; filtering image and video searches; and no filtering. To choose a setting, click the Advanced link on the Yahoo! home page. The Advanced Web Search page opens. Scroll down to the SafeSearch Filter area, where you can select your filtering preference. Note that this setting applies only to that search. To apply your setting to every search, click the Preferences link. This opens a new window called Search Preferences. You can adjust the setting for search filtering and then save the setting by clicking the Save Preferences button in the upper-right corner. The problem with this setting is that it can be easily turned off by anyone who uses the computer. Yahoo! also gives you the option to lock your search filter preferences, but you need to be a registered Yahoo! user. Simply click the Log In link, type in your Yahoo! username and password, choose your setting, and click a checkbox to lock SafeSearch in the mode you choose. You can then click Save Preferences. However, as Yahoo! mentions on the site, anyone who signs in to the computer as being 18 or older can simply bypass the Yahoo! settings.

- MSN Search offers three levels of filtering: Strict, which filters sexually explicit text and images; Moderate, which filters explicit images; and Off. Go to www.msn.com and click the Search button next to the search field. This opens a new window. Simply click the Settings button to choose your filtering level. You can save the setting, but there's no way to prevent anyone else who uses the computer from changing it.

Internet Explorer Filtering

You can get a stronger level of filtering by engaging Internet Explorer's capabilities. This avoids the problem of trying to manage settings on a large number of search engines (although I recommend setting up filters on the major search engines in addition to browser adjustments). However, note that the IE filtering system is cumbersome to set up and maintain, and the rating system has flaws.

IE has a browser filtering system called Content Advisor. Content Advisor uses a built-in rating system called RSACi (Recreational Software Advisory Council). However, according to the Web site for RSACi, this ratings system is now defunct and has been folded into the Internet Content Rating Association (ICRA). Content Advisor can also use the rating system from an organization called SafeSurf. We'll look at setting up Content Advisor to work with the ICRA.

The ICRA has developed a vocabulary that describes five general topics: Nudity and Sexual Content, Violence, Language, Chat Facilities, and a grab bag topic that includes gambling and drugs. Web site operators fill out a questionnaire that rates the Web site's content using 45 descriptions associated with the five topics. For instance, if a Web site has content that falls within the Nudity and Sexual Content topic, the site can indicate the presence of male and female genitalia and explicit sexual acts. Based on the results of the questionnaire, the ICRA generates a piece of code that the Web site operator attaches to the site. The Internet Explorer browser checks for this code and allows or denies access based on the settings you've chosen in Content Advisor.

Note that the ICRA does not seek out objectionable sites to label; Web site operators voluntarily participate in the program and fill out the questionnaire themselves. The obvious flaw in this system is that the ICRA can't do anything about sites that aren't labeled. My guess is that the vast majority of porn, violence, and gambling sites on the Internet are not labeled. (A quick check using the ICRA's own testing system shows that Playboy.com does have an ICRA label, but Penthouse.com does not.) In addition, there's very little to stop a Web site operator from falsifying information on a questionnaire.

SafeSurf uses a similar ratings system to cover a similar set of topics, including adult themes, heterosexual and homosexual themes, glorification of drug use, and violence. Like ICRA, SafeSurf is a voluntary system for Web site providers.

To use the ICRA ratings system inside the Content Advisor, you must first download a ratings file (called .rat for short). You have to download this file at www.icra.org/faq/contentadvisor/setup/. Select the Save option on the download screen. Then save it on your computer (if you are using Windows XP) to C:\WINDOWS\System32. This Web site is also a good tutorial for adjusting the settings of Content Advisor once you've added the ICRA .rat file.

Now it's time to set up Content Advisor in Internet Explorer. Select Tools, Internet Options. This opens the Internet Options window, as shown in Figure 8.5. Click the Content tab. Then click Enable in the Content Advisor section.

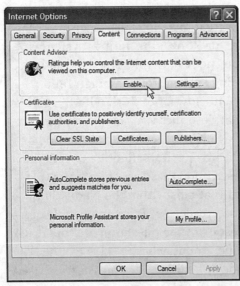

Figure 8.5   The Content tab of the Internet Options dialog box.

When you set up Content Advisor, it asks you to choose a password. This password makes you the Supervisor. As Supervisor you control the settings of Content Advisor, and you can allow or disallow specific sites. Make sure you pick a password you won't forget but also a password that your kids don't know.

> Both Microsoft and the ICRA strongly suggest that you be extra careful about this password, because if you forget it, you will not be able to turn off the content filtering system, and you may end up blocking access to sites you want. Neither Microsoft nor ICRA has a copy of this password, so they can't help you recover it if you lose it.

After you have chosen a password, you need to choose the ICRA .rat file. In the Internet Options dialog box (shown in Figure 8.5), click the Settings button. This opens a new window called Content Advisor, as shown in Figure 8.6. Click the General tab, and then click Rating Systems.... This opens a small window with options to add and remove rating systems, as shown in Figure 8.7. The RSACi system likely will be listed. You need to remove it, because it no longer works. You also have to add the ICRA .rat file you downloaded.

Figure 8.6   The General tab of the Content Advisor dialog box.

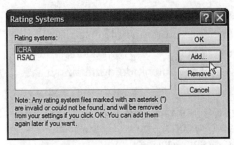

Figure 8.7 The Rating Systems dialog box.

To add the ICRA .rat file, click the Add button. This should open the system32 file, where you saved the ICRA file. Double-click the ICRA file. It should now be inside the Rating Systems box. Select the ICRA option and click OK.

Now proceed to the Ratings tab of the Content Advisor window, as shown in Figure 8.8. You should see ICRA listed. You can adjust the settings on dozens of categories, including Chat, Language, Nudity, and so on. If you click a category, a slider bar appears. It enables one of two settings: allow the category described or deny the category described. The default setting seems to be to deny. The Content Advisor doesn't support some categories, and the ICRA rating asks you to leave the slider bar all the way to the right.

Figure 8.8 The Ratings tab of the Content Advisor dialog box.

When you have adjusted each setting, click Apply. You can then go to the General tab to set up basic user options (see Figure 8.6). Note that because ICRA is a voluntary ratings system, Web sites may not participate, which means no ratings are available. You can configure Content Advisor to let users see sites that don't have a rating. Or you can configure it so that the Supervisor (that's you) has to type in a password to let users see unrated sites.

I tested the system to block all Web sites that don't have a rating. Some of the sites that were blocked because they don't have a rating include PBSKids.org, SesameStreet.com, ThomasTheTankEngine.com (yes, I have kids), StarWars.com, ESPN.com, eBay.com, CNN.com, and Yahoo.com.

As you can see, if you block all sites that don't have a rating, you block a lot of harmless sites along with sites containing explicit content. However, if you don't block unrated sites, a brief test shows that lots of pornography sites aren't rated, so Content Advisor lets them through if you've configured it not to block unrated sites.

What to do? One option is to preload the system with approved sites. You can do this by opening the Content Advisor window, clicking Settings, and then clicking the Approved Sites tab (see Figure 8.9). You then type the URLs of sites that will always be allowed. (You can also enter sites that will never be allowed.)

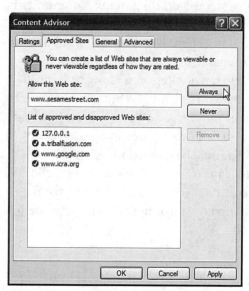

Figure 8.9   The Approved Sites tab of the Content Advisor dialog box.

Also, if you block unrated sites, the Supervisor has the option of moving blocked sites to the Allowed list using your Supervisor password. Each time the Content Advisor blocks a site, the Supervisor can make three selections: always allow the Web site to be viewed, always allow the specific Web page to be viewed, or allow viewing only during that session. You must enter the Supervisor password to enable any of these options.

Thus, if you use the Content Rating feature, you have to spend a lot of time putting allowed sites into this section. You may also frustrate your family members if they discover that a harmless site is blocked and you aren't around to unblock it. If you don't mind doing this, Content Advisor provides a very strong filtering mechanism for Internet Explorer. However, if you aren't prepared to pre-load allowed sites, and you don't like the idea of having to unblock unrated sites, Content Advisor won't be particularly effective at screening unwanted material.

Alternative Browser Filtering

As far as I can tell, popular alternative browsers, including Firefox and Opera (the free version), don't provide any built-in Web content filtering mechanisms. Therefore, if you have any of these browsers installed on your computer, your kids have a simple workaround to Content Advisor. However, the Firefox community is continually building extensions for the browser. At the time this chapter was written, I couldn't locate any projects for filtering objectionable Web content, but that may change. The closest thing I could find was an extension called Image-Show-Hide. According to the brief description, the extension lets you show or hide all images on all Web pages. However, the mechanism is simply a button that switches the extension on or off, so it's easy to get around. In addition, it doesn't actually filter objectionable content: If you have it turned on, it hides images on every Web page you visit, which is a bit extreme. To find the extension, go to https://addons.mozilla.org/, click the link for Firefox extensions, and then click the link for Image Browsing, which is located in a column on the left side of the page. You may also want to visit the extensions Web page now and then to see if a filtering extension has been written.

Service Provider Controls

Many service providers offer mechanisms for protecting children online and providing safe Web surfing. The best way to find out is to visit your provider's home page or call customer service. In the meantime, here's an outline of parental controls offered by three major service providers. You have to be a subscriber to actually get these services.

- AOL offers several parental control features, including AOL Guardian, which e-mails a "report card" to parents that shows e-mail, surfing, and instant messaging (IM) activities. Other features include a timing mechanism to control when and how long your kids can be online, a lock that prevents them from launching alternative browsers, and the ability to create a list of approved e-mail addresses. However, these features work only if your kids sign in with their own online identities. The easiest way to get around these restrictions is to use your ID and password. AOL also offers the KOL service, which is geared specifically for children and includes chat rooms monitored by AOL staffers. You have to subscribe to AOL for these services.

- Earthlink offers free parental controls with its dial-up and high-speed service options. At the top of the list is Web site filtering. You can either limit your kids to 15,000 sites that have been approved by Earthlink or give them full access to the Internet, except for 3 million sites that Earthlink blocks as part of its parental control system. Earthlink can also automatically remove offensive language from Web sites. Earthlink also offers a kid-friendly CyberFriends Communicator that includes e-mail, chat, bulletin board, and instant messaging functions. Parents can create a white list of people with whom their children can communicate. Parents can also review all the e-mails their children send and receive using the CyberFriends Communicator. Finally, parents can limit the amount of time kids spend online. As mentioned, these controls can be applied only if your kids sign in with their own online identity.

- The Children's Internet is an online service dedicated to children. It locks down the desktop so that kids can use only the features built into the service (it includes Web browsing, e-mail, and chat). If your kid has his or her own computer, this may be a good option. See www.childrensinternet.com for more information.

Spam Control

A lot of junk e-mail is pornographic or otherwise objectionable, and most spammers don't care that such material may end up in a kid's e-mail folder. A spam filtering solution can help weed out pornographic and sexually explicit junk mail from your kids' inboxes. See Chapter 6, "Just Say No to Spam," for more information on dealing with spam.

In addition, you can report spammers who send pornographic junk e-mail to your kids. To file a report, go to the Web site for the National Center for Missing and Exploited Children (www.missingkids.com). Click the CyberTipline link on the left side of the page, scroll down to the Unsolicited Obscene Material Sent to a Child heading, and then click the Report button. Your report may not result in an immediate investigation, but if enough complaints get registered, you may help get a spammer thrown in jail.

8.2 Sexual Predators and the Internet

An unfortunate fact of modern life is that sexual predators use the Internet—especially online chat rooms—to seek out potential victims. According to a 2000 report by the Crimes Against Children Research Center, nearly one out of five young Internet users surveyed received unwanted sexual solicitation. Even more disturbing, 3 percent of those surveyed reported receiving an "aggressive solicitation" for offline contact. Nearly a quarter of the children who'd been solicited were between the ages of 10 and 13, while 77 percent were between 14 and 17 years old. (See the "Helpful Resources" section for a link to this report.)

This problem is exacerbated because kids may be less cautious on the Internet than they would in the real world, in part because the Internet provides a false sense of anonymity and safety. Thus, they may be emboldened to engage in conversations or relationships that they wouldn't in person. In addition, younger children are susceptible to manipulation and may develop a misplaced trust in online "friends."

But before you yank the phone cord from the back of the computer, you can take steps to protect your kids while they are online. First and foremost, talk with them. Use age-appropriate language to discuss the problem, and encourage them to come to you if they encounter anything on the Internet that makes them uncomfortable. Also be sure to keep an eye on what your children do while they're online. As discussed earlier, you can do this with both physical monitoring and by using third-party software. We'll go into more details about the problem of inappropriate contact and possible solutions in the remainder of this section.

Preventing Unwanted Contact

By knowing how sexual predators operate, you can better communicate the danger signs to your kids. And if you're monitoring your kids' online activities, you'll recognize suspicious communications right away.

According to the FBI, sexual predators are most likely to roam chat rooms to establish connections with kids. The open nature of chat rooms makes it easy to initiate online conversations, which usually begin with innocuous discussions about popular culture, music, and other topics of interest to kids. Over time, predators may establish a rapport by providing attention, affection, empathy, and even offers of gifts. Once the predator has gained the child's trust, he or she may attempt to move additional conversations to more private media, such as e-mail, instant messaging, and even telephone calls. At this point, he or she begins to introduce sexual topics or share explicit materials, including child pornography. Predators may eventually try to arrange meetings with potential victims; the FBI has reported that one would-be victimizer mailed airplane tickets to encourage a meeting.

It's tempting to simply forbid access to chat rooms, but this isn't a realistic solution given the proliferation of Internet access. Kids can get online at school, at the library, at a friend's house, at public kiosks at Internet cafes, and at home when you're not there. In addition, instant messaging and chat can be a good and useful way for kids to communicate and develop social skills. So rather than pull the plug, use the following tips to help you keep your own home computers safe and teach your kids how to be smart Internet users:

- Talk with your children about the potential dangers on the Internet. Ask them to tell you if they have any contact that makes them uncomfortable. If you're not sure how to begin such a discussion, check out NetSmartz.org, which is sponsored by the Center for Missing and Exploited Children. NetSmartz.org has information about online safety for both young children and teenagers, and it's a great resource for parents.

- Instruct your children not to reveal their names, ages, addresses, or phone numbers in chat rooms, e-mail, IM, and so on. They should also refrain from posting photos of themselves online.

- If you can, have your home computer in a high-traffic area in the house, such as the living room. Monitor your children's online activity, including e-mail and Web sites they've visited.

- Watch for danger signs, as outlined in the sidebar "Signs Your Child Might Be at Risk Online" at the end of this chapter.

- Take advantage of parental control features available from your service provider, in browsers and search engines, and in third-party software.

Reporting Sexual Solicitation

The FBI recommends that you file a report if your child or anyone else in your household has received child pornography, if your child under age 18 is solicited sexually by someone who knows the child is under 18, or if your child under 18 has received explicit images from someone who knows your child is under 18.

You can report these crimes to local law enforcement and the FBI. (You can call 202-324-3000. To find the field office nearest you, go to www.fbi.gov/contact/fo/fo.htm.) You can also use the CyberTipline located on the left side of the National Center for Missing and Exploited Children's home page at www.missingkids.com to report the incident.

The FBI also notes that if any of these scenarios occur and you report it, you should turn off your computer and leave it alone. Do not delete or make copies of files or images. A law enforcement agent will take the computer for forensic examination, a process that could take days or weeks.

Internet Monitoring Software

In addition to talking with your kids about potential dangers, Internet monitoring software can help you enforce restrictions and keep a close eye on your kids' online activity. Some people may regard spying on their children's Internet activity as invasive and another symptom of the American malady of hyper-parenting. Others may view it as an appropriate precaution, like bicycle helmets and seat belts. The lengths you go to to restrict and monitor activity will depend on a variety of factors, including the age of your children (older kids are likely to be savvier and can get around simple search engine and browser filters); your own assessment of the risks they face; and the amount of time, effort, and money you're willing to invest.

The section "Filtering Unwanted Content" looked at easy and free filters. This section looks at software that was designed to enforce parental controls and provide a window into your kids' Web usage. This category of software provides more comprehensive controls and offers a larger set of features than the options discussed earlier, but you'll have to pay for these expanded capabilities.

How Should I Choose?

There are several criteria for choosing Internet monitoring software. The first is the comprehensiveness of the controls. The most likely areas you'll want some control over include Web browsing and online chat and instant messaging. A comprehensive product should be able to filter the major Web browsers and IM programs. A good product should also address image searches in search engines, either by filtering objectionable search results or by locking a user into a pre-screened search engine that does not return objectionable results. You may also be interested in filtering and monitoring e-mail.

When evaluating a program, keep in mind the differences between filtering and monitoring. Filtering blocks objectionable content or replaces it with Xs or periods. Monitoring lets you review information to find out what your kids are doing online (for instance, seeing which Web sites they visited or recording complete IM conversations).

Besides the specific controls, you should also be aware of the different filtering methods, particularly with Web content. The simplest system is a blacklist of Web site URLs that contain objectionable content, or of keywords that indicate objectionable material. These blacklists are usually maintained by the company that makes the parental control software. They likely cover a range of categories, including pornography, violence, alcohol and drug use, and so on. Blacklists are effective as long as the list is comprehensive. However, given the size and mutability of the Internet, new sites continually emerge and old sites vanish into the ether. Thus, when comparing products, look for systems that regularly update their lists. Most systems also let you add your own sets of restricted and allowed sites.

Another option is to scan the Web site before it gets displayed in the browser. This scan may look for objectionable language or, if images are present, attempt to assess the kind of image (for instance, by examining images for faces, shapes, and skin). Of the products listed in Table 8.1, EnoLogic NetFilter Home uses image analysis to block pornographic images in real time. Image analysis is useful for detecting objectionable content without resorting to a blacklist, but it can also block harmless sites. You may want to look for a solution that allows immediate parental override to allow sites that have been mistakenly blocked.

Most parental control software also allows you to limit the time your kids spend online, block or filter IM and chat, prevent programs from downloading files, and prevent kids from entering personal information such as phone numbers.

Some security programs come with limited parental controls built in. Norton Internet Security, which bundles a firewall, anti-virus, anti-spyware, and other important security features, also includes some Parental Control settings to block access to unwanted content. When activated, it can block Web sites based on a list of categories maintained by Symantec, including sex, nudity, drug abuse, and violence. Conversely, you can also restrict users to a list of allowed Web sites and block everything else. (This setting may be overkill, at least for older children, for whom it would be impossible to anticipate every site they might need access to.) You can also block specific programs from accessing the Internet and restrict newsgroups.

Note that all parental control software is based on user accounts that are created for each person who uses your computer. If your children know an adult's account name and password, they can bypass these parental controls (assuming you've granted the adults unfiltered access). Some products offer a stealth mechanism so that your kids won't see the product's icon in the system tray. A stealth setting may be useful if you have older, computer-savvy kids who might be inclined to try to get around your restrictions.

The products listed in Table 8.1 represent only a small number of software solutions for parental controls. You can find helpful reviews of parental control software at *PC Magazine* (www.pcmagazine.com) and at http://internet-filter-review.toptenreviews.com/. As of mid-2005, prices for standalone parental control software range from $29.95 to $55. Note that special promotions or rebates may affect the final cost.

8.3 The $3,000 Song and Other File-Sharing Problems

A recurring theme of this book is that money drives a majority of the security problems we face when using the Internet. That's also the case in this section, but with a twist: Rather than your being the victim of savvy Internet criminals, two gigantic organizations feel that *they* are the victims and *you* are the thief. Well, maybe not you personally, but anyone who uses the Internet to find, download, and share copyrighted music and movies without paying a dime in licenses or royalties. These organizations, the Recording Industry Association of America (RIAA) and the

Table 8.1

Selected Parental Control Software

Product	Vendor	Web Site	Features
ContentProtect	ContentWatch	www.contentwatch.com	Real-time Web site analysis, blocks access to chat, time limits, activity log, password override, and more.
CyberPatrol	SurfControl	www.cyberpatrol.com	Web site blacklists and white lists, real-time Web site text analysis, search engine image result filtering, chat and IM blocking, time limits, blocks spyware sites, and more.
CYBERSitter	Solid Oak Software	www.cybersitter.com	Web site blacklists and white lists, search engine image blocking, time limits, records IM conversations on AOL and Yahoo! Messenger, stealth mode, and more.
EnoLogic NetFilter Home	EnoLogic	www.enologic.com	Image and text analysis for Web sites, user blacklisting, blocks chat, blocks private information, blocks large file transfers, detects MP3 files, and more.
NetNanny	LookSmart	www.netnanny.com	Web site blacklists and white lists, activity log, text filtering on browsers, chat, e-mail, and newsgroups, time limits, blocks access to chat and IM, and more.

Motion Picture Association of America (MPAA), claim that they lose millions of dollars in record and movie sales because of a technology called file sharing.

File-sharing technology does what it says: It allows users to share files. The vast majority of those files tend to be music files, usually in the form of MP3, which is a format for encoding and compressing audio signals. Other popular digital formats include Windows Media Audio (WMA), which Microsoft uses, and Advanced Audio Coding (AAC), used by Apple's iTunes store and iPod players. File-sharing programs also let you share any other kind of digital file, including movies, documents, photos, and software programs.

File sharing generally takes place over peer-to-peer (P2P) networks. P2P networks consist of individual nodes, such as PCs, that are connected across a network. P2P networks stand in contrast to client/server networks. In a client/server network, a group of clients sends and receives data to and from a central server. This server may be configured to allow the clients to share the same files or resources, but the clients do not communicate with each other individually; the server is the master repository of information. Your office network is most likely built on a client/server model.

By contrast, a peer-to-peer network doesn't have a master server; each node, or peer, on the network can download files from other peers and serve files to other peers. The larger P2P networks have index nodes that tell which files are available on which peers, and they can rank peers by their network capacity.

Napster was the first P2P network to receive significant public attention. It was also one of the first major P2P networks to come under legal fire from the recording industry. It sued Napster for enabling copyright infringement because so many people used Napster to download and share songs without paying for them. Napster was eventually shut down, but it has reemerged as an online music store that pays the appropriate royalties to the recording industry.

However, in regard to file sharing and P2P, the digital cat is out of the bag. P2P networks such as Kazaa, Grokster, Gnutella, Morpheus, and hundreds of others enable users to find and share music, movies, and other digital content for free.

Of course, that isn't stopping the RIAA from trying to stuff the cat back in. At this point in its efforts, the RIAA doesn't have technology on its side; various attempts to encrypt and otherwise protect digital audio from being copied and distributed have failed. However, the RIAA does have the law on its side: downloading or making available for download copyrighted content without the permission of the copyright holder is illegal. However, P2P software is not illegal, which is where things begin to get complicated.

The RIAA and the MPAA are pursuing their legal battle on two fronts. First, they are going after the P2P software makers that enable copyright violation. Second, they are going after organizations (in particular, universities) and individuals who illegally share copyrighted content.

In April 2005, the RIAA announced a new round of lawsuits against individuals who are allegedly guilty of illegal file sharing. One blogger says this round brings the total number of people sued by the RIAA to more than 10,000 (see http://sharenomore.blogspot.com/). In 2003, the RIAA sued hundreds of people for illegally sharing copyrighted music. The average fine was approximately $3,000.

The MPAA is also pursuing file swappers. It launched an initial round of lawsuits in November 2004, and it followed up with a second round in January 2005.

In April 2005, President George W. Bush signed into law the new Family Entertainment and Copyright Act. Designed to up the ante against digital pirates, the law says that anyone caught with a prerelease movie, song, or software program on his or her computer could face as much as three years in jail or fines of up to $250,000.

Finally, the Supreme Court began hearing arguments in the case of *MGM Studios, Inc. v. Grokster, LTD* in the early spring of 2005. The gist of the argument is that MGM, a movie studio, claims that Grokster, a P2P file-sharing program, is liable for all the copyright violations it enables by providing users with a mechanism to share copyrighted material. The case is complex and likely will involve a good deal of deliberation before the Court makes its ruling. Many observers are citing the precedent set by *Sony v. Universal Studios*, in which Universal sued Sony for copyright violation, saying that Sony's Betamax technology enabled consumers to illegally record television programs. The Supreme Court ruled against Universal, saying that Sony was not liable for what consumers did with the technology. The Court also noted that consumers' actions (recording TV shows to watch later) constituted fair use of copyrighted material.

In the current case, however, it may be difficult to argue that sharing copyrighted songs with a potential audience of millions constitutes fair use, given the significant potential for lost income on the part of the copyright holders. At the time this chapter was written, the Supreme Court had not ruled on the case. See the "Helpful Resources" section for a link that provides a great overview of the case and the potential repercussions of possible Court rulings.

How Can They Find Me?

The Internet provides a false sense of anonymity for users of P2P software. As the number of lawsuits filed by the RIAA and MPAA show, individual users can and are found. The question is not whether they can find you, but whether you will be one of the people caught in their semi-regular sweeps of copyright violators. Currently these organizations are going after the most egregious users, so the chances of your being targeted by one of these organizations is low (assuming you haven't set up a Web server bristling with digital audio files).

So how do they find copyright violators? Well, the most obvious way they do it is to sign on to various P2P networks and find nodes that are sharing copyright-ed content. The RIAA and MPAA have their own criteria for deciding which nodes to pursue, but once they've decided which ones to go after, they verify that in fact the node is illegally hosting copyrighted material. Then they can find out the node's IP address using various lookup tools. Once they have the IP address, they can determine the node's service provider. Then they simply file a "John Doe" lawsuit. According to information on the RIAA's Web site, plaintiffs can file "John Doe" lawsuits when they don't know the name of the person they are suing. Once the lawsuit is filed, the plaintiff can subpoena the ISP to get the name of the person using that IP address. For more information, see www.riaa.com/news/newsletter/012104_faq.asp.

In its earlier lawsuits the RIAA tried to do this process the other way around; that is, it tried to subpoena the ISPs into giving out the name and personal infor-mation of the copyright infringer so that the RIAA could then file a lawsuit against that person. However, Verizon Online challenged the RIAA's subpoena. The RIAA then sued Verizon, and the case went all the way to the Supreme Court, which let stand a previous ruling saying service providers can keep the identity of their customers' secret. That said, the John Doe lawsuit process is entirely legal, which means that if an ISP is served a subpoena as part of a John Doe lawsuit, it must turn over the subscriber's name and personal information.

P2P Security Issues

In addition to the potential legal troubles that come from not paying for music and movies, P2P programs can expose you to security risks. When you download and use P2P software, you may not realize that you are exposing your computer to other computers on the Internet. A particular folder that contains digital files to share may be open to the Internet. If it's improperly configured, you could open your entire hard drive and all its contents to the Internet. If you're using a firewall (and if you've made it this far through the book, you should have one installed), you have to open ports to let the P2P software work. However, by opening these ports you expose your computer to nefarious intruders.

In addition, as discussed in Chapter 6, most P2P applications also include adware that may track your online behavior, generate annoying pop-up ads, and degrade your computer's performance. Finally, attackers and criminals have taken to planting Trojan horses and other malware inside P2P files and giving them interesting or enticing names. You think you're getting a cool U2 B side or a copy of the *Hitchhiker's Guide to the Galaxy* movie, but instead you've installed a keystroke logger on your computer.

If you still want to use P2P software, make sure you use anti-virus and anti-spyware software to scan all the files you download, and read the configuration instructions carefully to ensure that the only files you expose to the Internet are the ones you actually want to share. As mentioned, most P2P programs set up a specific folder on your computer for this purpose.

Legal or Illegal?

Confused by all the legal wrangling over file sharing? Table 8.2 is a quick guide to help you sort out what's right and what might get you sued or arrested.

Table 8.2

Legal Versus Illegal File Sharing	
Legal	**Illegal**
Using P2P software.	Using P2P software to download and share copyrighted material without permission.
Buying music online.	Buying music online and then sharing it via P2P software.
Copying digital audio or movie files that you've paid for onto a CD or portable player.	Copying audio or movie files to resell them or share them on P2P networks.

8.4 Checklist

Use this checklist as a quick-reference guide to the material covered in this chapter.

Do

- Take advantage of filtering options to screen out objectionable Internet content.
- Try and limit your children's Internet usage to a computer located in a high-traffic area such as the living room or kitchen.
- Talk to your children about the potential dangers of the Internet.
- Encourage your children not to post their names, phone numbers, home addresses, e-mail addresses, and photographs on the Web.
- Watch for signs that your child may have been approached by a sexual predator online.
- Talk to your children about the legal and security issues associated with peer-to-peer file sharing.

Don't

- Let your children use the Internet without supervision.
- Believe that filtering systems are 100 percent effective.
- Believe that your filtering system can't be gotten around.

8.5 Helpful Resources

This section presents additional resources to help you learn more.

The National Center for Missing and Exploited Children is a nonprofit organization that provides services to families with missing, abused, or sexually exploited children. The Center's Web site, www.missingkids.com, has lots of information about protecting children online. Also, if you need to report online sexual solicitation or other issues, the Web site's CyberTipline is an excellent place to start. You can find the link to the CyberTipline on the left side of the home page.

To read the report "Online Victimization: A Report on the Nation's Youth" by the Crimes Against Children Research Center, go to www.missingkids.com/en_US/publications/NC62.pdf.

For more information about how to talk about online safety with your kids or teenagers, go to www.netsmartz.org. Young kids can also view the www.netsmartzkids.org site for an online tutorial about Internet safety. NetSmartz is cosponsored by the National Center for Missing and Exploited Children and the Boys and Girls Clubs of America.

"A Parent's Guide to Internet Safety," published by the FBI, provides helpful tips for keeping your children safe online. It also outlines the steps to take if you suspect your child is communicating with a sexual predator. Go to www.fbi.gov/publications/pguide/pguidee.htm to read the guide.

To read more about music piracy from the perspective of the Recording Industry Association of America (RIAA), go to www.riaa.com/issues/piracy/default.asp. You may want to check out the Penalties link in the upper-right corner.

Julie Hilden has written an excellent overview of the *MGM v. Grokster* case currently before the Supreme Court. You can read it at www.cnn.com/2005/LAW/02/16/hilden.fileswap/.

Signs Your Child Might Be at Risk Online

Despite your vigilance, it's possible for kids to encounter sexual predators or disturbing sexual materials online. The FBI has outlined seven signs that may indicate your child is at risk online. The seven signs listed here are paraphrased from "A Parent's Guide to Internet Safety" by the FBI. You can find a link to the full guide in the "Helpful Resources" section. While these signs are useful, parents should keep in mind that two of these signs (spending lots of time on the Internet and isolating oneself from the family) can be completely normal behavior, particularly for pre-teens and teenagers. If you suspect there's a problem, talk with your children before jumping to conclusions.

- Your child spends a lot of time using the Internet. Just how much time is "a lot" varies from family to family, so you have to use your best judgment. However, the FBI states that child predators are most active in the evenings and on weekends.

continues . . .

- You find pornography on your child's computer. Sexual predators may use pornography, including child pornography, to begin sexual discussions with children or to seduce potential victims. If you discover that someone has sent pornography (especially child pornography) to your child, you should contact your local law enforcement and the FBI. (Call 202-324-3000 or go to www.fbi.gov/contact/fo/fo.htm to find the field office nearest you.) You can also use the CyberTipline located on the left side of the home page at www.missingkids.com to report the incident. If you are reporting pornography to law enforcement, the FBI recommends that you shut down your computer and leave it alone. Be aware that a law enforcement officer or agent likely will remove your computer to conduct a forensic investigation.

- Your child receives phone calls from strangers or makes calls to unknown numbers. Sexual predators often try to move communication from chat rooms to more private media. Some predators attempt to engage children in phone sex or use the phone to set up an in-person meeting.

- A stranger sends your child mail, gifts, or packages. Sexual predators may pursue additional communication and use gifts to help establish rapport.

- Your child turns off the computer or quickly switches to a different screen when you enter the room. This is a sign that your child may be looking at something you wouldn't want him or her to see.

- Your child withdraws from the family. A sexual predator may try to isolate your child from the rest of the family to facilitate manipulating his or her relationship with the child. In the worst-case scenario, this may be a sign that your child has already been victimized.

- Your child uses alternative online accounts. While you may have access to your child's primary online account, it's incredibly easy for your child to set up e-mail and instant-message accounts that you may not know about. These separate accounts may be benign, but they can also be used for private communication between a predator and a potential victim.

To see a full copy of the FBI's guide to safe Internet surfing for families, which includes these danger signs, see the "Helpful Resources" section.

Chapter 9

Wireless and VoIP Security

It used to be that computers were computers and phones were phones. These days the distinction is harder to make, and within the next five years it likely will be meaningless. Thanks to developments in wireless computing and Internet telephony, today's PCs are more mobile than ever, and you can even place a phone call from your computer. Meanwhile, cell phones, personal digital assistants (PDAs), and wireless e-mail devices are packing on the features, functions, and processing power of desktop computers.

These developments have a lot of upsides. Wireless technology offers increased mobility and convenience at home, and makes it easier to connect to the Internet outside the home. For the time being, wireless computing is limited to a few public "hotspots." Eventually, however, you'll enjoy the same kind of widespread wireless Internet coverage for your computer that you get from your cell phone provider. Voice over IP (VoIP) currently offers cheap phone service by transforming your computer into a telephone and routing your phone calls over the Internet.

And speaking of phones, the cellular versions are also undergoing phenomenal developments as vendors add features and services such as text messaging (who would've thought that using a telephone to send a readable message would become so popular?), digital photos, and Internet access. In addition, devices such as the BlackBerry, which provide wireless e-mail on the go, and Palm Pilots, which are digital organizers, will incorporate telephone features, further blurring the lines among handheld communication devices. And in the future (at least the one dreamed up by advertisers), local businesses will beam coupons and sale offers to your cell phone as you walk past their stores.

Of course, as you should have guessed by now, the good parts of any technology must be weighed against the potential security drawbacks. And the drawbacks, particularly in the case of wireless, are significant. Problems range from wireless freeloaders who latch on to your Internet connection and surf for free to thieves and criminals who are out to steal sensitive information. As cell phones morph into handheld computers, they will fall prey to many of the problems that plague PCs (cell phone viruses are already here). And as your computer turns into a phone via VoIP, that transformation has its own drawbacks, some of which may have safety implications (911 service). This chapter looks at the potential dangers of these new technologies.

9.1 How Wireless Networks Work

Today, many households have more than one computer requiring a simultaneous Internet connection. Thus, home networks are springing up all across the country. A home network links multiple computers so that they can exchange files and share Internet access. Home networks can be wired or wireless. Wireless networks are popular because you don't have to run cables to every computer in the house, and your family can simultaneously share an Internet connection from bedrooms, the living room, the home office, and even outdoors (depending on the strength of the access point).

A basic wireless connection requires two components: a wireless card or chip in your computer, and an access point (AP), which is sometimes called a wireless router. Today, most laptops come with wireless capability built into the machine itself. If you have an older laptop, you can buy a wireless card to add wireless capability. The access point hooks up to whatever mechanism you use to connect to the Internet: a phone jack, DSL modem, or cable modem. Multiple computers can connect over the airwaves to a single access point. The major vendors of home wireless network products include Linksys, Belkin, D-Link, and NetGear.

Today's home wireless networks are based on a set of standards collectively known as Wi-Fi, which is short for wireless fidelity. Wi-Fi is governed by the Institute of Electrical and Electronics Engineers (IEEE), which oversees technology standards in part to ensure that products from different companies interoperate. Wi-Fi consists of a variety of standards that are described using a numeric system called 802.11, which is the name of the committee that creates wireless networking standards. This chapter is concerned with four IEEE standards: 802.11b, 802.11g, 802.11a, and 802.1x. The b, g, and a standards address basic issues about data transmission. 802.1x describes a framework for exchanging authentication information among devices in a wireless network. You'll learn more about 802.1x later in this chapter.

The b, g, and a standards are different in several ways, including capacity (how much data they can transmit at what speed), range (how far the signal can travel), what portion of the radio spectrum they use, and how they deal with problems of interference. (Radio signals suffer interference from physical objects such as walls, beams, and natural features like hills, as well as from electromagnetic waves generated by other devices such as microwave ovens.)

The 802.11b standard is the most widely adopted, which means that a majority of the wireless equipment you buy uses or supports this standard. It also means that many public hotspots, such as at cafes, use this standard. 802.11b has a maximum capacity rating of 11 megabits per second and can send and receive data up to 150 feet. However, the newer standards offer greater speed—up to 54 megabits per second—but they aren't yet as widely supported by products (a fact that will rapidly change). That said, new products are emerging all the time, and some support multiple standards and can switch among them, depending on the network's requirements. Choosing a standard means accepting various trade-offs. For instance, 802.11a has only half the range of the others, but it operates in the 5 GHz spectrum, which is less crowded and thus less prone to electromagnetic interference. 802.11b and g have greater speed and are available in many consumer Wi-Fi products and public wireless networks. However, they may experience interference from cordless phones and microwave ovens. Table 9.1 summarizes the three Wi-Fi standards.

9.2 Security Issues with Home WLANs

The convenience of Wi-Fi networks (also called Wireless Local Area Networks, or WLANs) comes with a price: a serious lack of privacy and security. You may not realize it, but the wireless card or chip in your computer and your access point are actually radios, albeit small ones that use different frequencies than the traditional AM/FM kind. The signals sent by your wireless devices can be picked up by any device within range, not just your own access point. Attackers know this, and they use software programs called sniffers, which allow them to eavesdrop on

Table 9.1

Wireless Network Standards				
Standard	Maximum Speed	Range	Product Support	Frequency
802.11b	11 megabits per second	100 to 150 feet	Widespread support in wireless products.	2.4 GHz
802.11g	54 megabits per second	100 to 150 feet	Growing product support. Is backward-compatible with 802.11b (though only at 11 megabits per second).	2.4 GHz
802.11a	54 megabits per second	25 to 75 feet	New technology with the least product support (so far). Does not interoperate with 802.11b or g.	5 GHz

unencrypted wireless connections. These sniffers are the wireless equivalent of listening in on a phone line, except that they can pick up your e-mail, your instant-messaging conversations, and of course any passwords or account numbers you might use during a wireless session. Wireless sniffing tools are updated versions of wired sniffing tools, which can monitor transmissions on wired networks. However, wireless sniffers are a lot easier to use because you don't have to tap a wire or find a spare network jack—you simply turn it on near a Wi-Fi network and watch the traffic flow.

In addition to sniffers, any other computers with a wireless card or chip in range can connect to your access point. Most WLAN technology has a maximum range of 150 feet, so your signal isn't traveling to China and back, but it certainly travels far enough for your neighbors or someone sitting in front of your house to pick up. Also keep in mind that wireless transmissions don't simply travel in a straight line; they radiate up, down, and outward like three-dimensional ripples on a pond. Wireless signals also pass through walls, floors, and ceilings, so neighbors above, below, and all around you may be within range.

Let's be clear that the risks you face using a home WLAN aren't all that severe. Chances are pretty low that a criminal will hang around outside your house and try to capture your wireless traffic. (The chance that this will happen is much greater at a public hotspot, but we'll address that issue later.) What's more likely is that a nosy neighbor could snoop on your traffic or use your Internet connection for free. Also, some wireless enthusiasts may drive around the neighborhood using special software to look for wireless networks. This is called war driving (which is a play on the term "war dialing," an attacker technique in which an automated computer program dials long lists of phone numbers looking for computer modems). War drivers may be looking for free Internet access in their neighborhood, but some war drivers are looking to break into networks. However, they are more likely to be attracted to corporate WLANs, many of which have little or no security in place.

While some people leave their APs open to promote widespread Internet access, if you prefer privacy you can lock down your WLAN. First, take advantage of the encryption mechanisms available with the access points. Encryption takes the data you send from your computer to the AP (and vice versa) and scrambles it into illegible text. This prevents other users from seeing everything you send and receive on your wireless connection.

There are three general mechanisms for encrypting WLAN traffic: WEP (Wired Equivalent Privacy), WPA (Wi-Fi Protected Access), and WPA2 (an updated version of WPA that uses a stronger encryption algorithm). WPA2 is the interoperable specification for 802.11i, yet another wireless standard that aims to improve the security of wireless networks.

WEP emerged with early versions of wireless networks and proved to be almost universally useless, particularly for securing business WLANs. The biggest problem with WEP is its poor use of encryption technology; that is, it uses short encryption keys over a long period of time. A key is a mathematical function that transforms plain text into gibberish, or ciphertext, and then transforms ciphertext back to plain text. Keys can be of varying lengths, from 40 bits to 2048 bits and beyond. Generally speaking, the longer the key, the harder it is for a computer to decipher an encrypted message by trying every possible combination of letters and numbers. However, longer keys also require more processing power to run the encryption and decryption functions, so shorter keys are used as a trade-off to improve operational speed. Some programs that use short keys also change them frequently (say every minute) so that if an attacker breaks one key, he or she has to start all over again when the new key begins operating.

Because WEP used a short key for a long period, and also implemented the key poorly, researchers soon discovered that with a little time and some help from a computer, an attacker could decipher WEP-encrypted transmissions. Software tools soon appeared on the Internet to attack WLANs. The most infamous, known as AirSnort, has been shown to crack WEP-protected transmissions in minutes.

WPA and WPA2 address WEP's shortcomings by using longer keys and changing those keys more frequently. If you're buying a wireless AP today, it uses

WPA or WPA2; older WLAN equipment may require a software upgrade from WEP to WPA. However, if an upgrade isn't available, you should still use WEP, because some protection is better than nothing. (WEP is useless for corporate networks, which are much more likely to be targeted by criminals and have lots of sensitive information floating around. However, WEP is sufficient to keep your neighbor from snooping on your wireless traffic.)

WPA and WPA2 have different modes for business users and home users. Home users should select the WPA-PSK (Wi-Fi Protected Access Preshared Key) option when setting up a wireless AP. WPA-PSK requires you to set a pass phrase that the AP uses to generate an encryption key. A good pass phrase uses both numbers and letters. You also enter this pass phrase in each device you want to connect to the AP. Once WPA is engaged, all communications between your computer and the AP are encrypted.

Windows XP Service Pack 2 (SP2) has a Wireless Network Setup Wizard to help you configure a WLAN. To find the wizard, click Start, and then choose Control Panel and Network and Internet Connections. You see the Wireless Network Setup Wizard next to an icon of a wireless card, as shown in Figure 9.1.

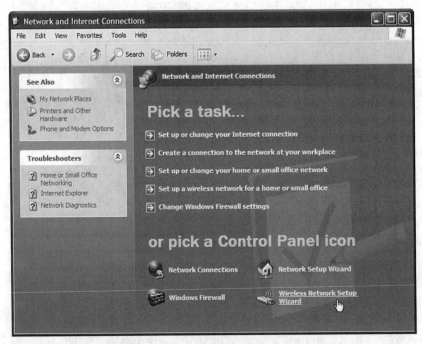

Figure 9.1   Accessing the Wireless Network Setup Wizard.

The wizard walks you through all the steps necessary to create a secure wireless network. The first screen asks you to choose an SSID (discussed in the next section), as shown in Figure 9.2. It also asks you whether you want to automatically or manually assign a network key. This is an encryption key that protects your communication. Microsoft recommends the automatic setting. If your access point supports WPA, check the box at the bottom of the screen to use WPA encryption instead of WEP.

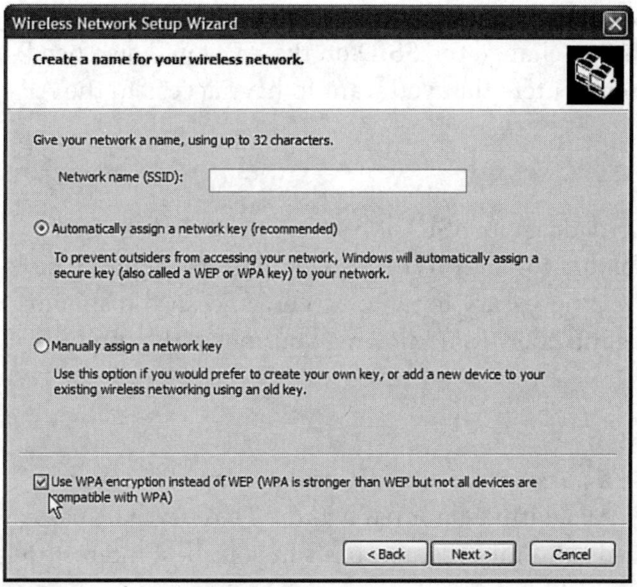

Figure 9.2   Choosing the SSID and WPA.

In addition to encryption, another security mechanism for wireless networks is 802.1x. This standard is a framework for sending authentication information, such as passwords, digital certificates, or security tokens, to give you access to a wireless network. You don't have to worry about 802.1x when setting up a home network, but you may encounter the standard if you buy time on a public wireless network, such as at a cafe or hotel.

You can also take additional steps to secure your Wi-Fi network, which we'll cover in the next sections.

Change the Default SSID

The SSID (Service Set Identifier) is a 32-character identifier for a wireless access point. An SSID basically acts as a network name to distinguish your AP or WLAN from other APs. Any device that wants to connect to your AP must know the SSID. The problem is that most vendors ship APs from the factory with the same default SSID (for instance, "default"). These factory SSIDs are well known, so you need to change it. You can choose any name you like for the SSID, but the best idea is to use a combination of words and letters. SSIDs are usually sent over the air unencrypted, so don't use sensitive information such as your birthday, Internet passwords, name, or address. If you change the SSID on the AP, you'll also need to enter the same SSID on any computers that you want to have access to the AP.

Turn Off SSID Broadcast

Your AP may be configured to broadcast its SSID at regular intervals (say, every few seconds). This is a useful feature for large WLANs where users might be moving from one AP to another. It's unnecessary for a home network, so you should turn it off to prevent a would-be intruder from knowing your network name.

Change Default Passwords

APs may also ask you to choose a password to change any settings. However, as with SSIDs, many vendors ship APs with default passwords. These default passwords are well known to criminals and miscreants, so it's in your best interest to change them.

Turn on MAC Filtering

Some access points let you configure the AP so that only computers with a specific MAC address are allowed to connect to it. (Note that the MAC address has nothing to do with Macintosh computers, which are often called Macs for short. MAC stands for Media Access Control.) A MAC address is a unique number given to every Network Interface Card (NIC)—no two NICs have the same number. A NIC, sometimes called an Ethernet card, is used to connect computers to computer networks. Most computers sold in the last few years include a NIC. Because every MAC address is unique, MAC filtering is an effective way to block unknown computers from using your WLAN.

To find your MAC address, click the Start button, select Run, and type **command**. This opens a DOS window with a blinking C prompt. Type **ipconfig/all** next to the C prompt and press Enter. The computer returns a list of specifications about the computer, as shown in Figure 9.3. Look for the entry called Physical Address. This is your MAC address. A MAC address uses both numbers and letters and should look something like 00.0D.60.FE.0F.1B. If your computer doesn't have a NIC, you can't use MAC filtering.

```
 C:\WINDOWS\system32\command.com                                    _ □ ×

Microsoft(R) Windows DOS
(C)Copyright Microsoft Corp 1990-2001.

C:\DOCUME~1\DREW>ipconfig/all

Windows IP Configuration

        Host Name . . . . . . . . . . . . : CONRY-MURRAY
        Primary Dns Suffix  . . . . . . . : HIP.Berkeley.EDU
        Node Type . . . . . . . . . . . . : Unknown
        IP Routing Enabled. . . . . . . . : No
        WINS Proxy Enabled. . . . . . . . : No
        DNS Suffix Search List. . . . . . : Berkeley.EDU
                                            HIP.Berkeley.EDU

Ethernet adapter Local Area Connection:

        Media State . . . . . . . . . . . : Media disconnected
        Description . . . . . . . . . . . : Intel(R) PRO/100 VE Network Connecti
on
        Physical Address. . . . . . . . . : 00-00-39-10-F7-DF

PPP adapter AT&T Connection Service:

        Connection-specific DNS Suffix  . :
```

Figure 9.3   A computer's MAC address.

Wireless Security Software

If you activate WPA and follow the other steps for securing your wireless connection, you are probably more secure than most of the people around you. This is good, because Internet criminals tend to be opportunistic: They go after unprotected targets first.

However, if you want extra security, you can buy wireless security programs. The real value of these extra programs is the help they offer when you connect to other wireless networks, such as at a cafe or hotspot.

Security software vendor McAfee offers a free scan to check the security of the wireless network connection you are using. The test downloads an ActiveX control to your computer to conduct the check, so you have to use the Internet Explorer browser to initiate the check. To run the test, go to www.mcafee.com. Click the section for home users and look under the Free Services section for McAfee Wi-Fi Scan.

Trend Micro has added Wi-Fi Intrusion Detection to PC-cillin, which also includes a personal firewall, anti-virus (AV) software, and anti-spyware software. The Wi-Fi Intrusion Detection module warns you when a war driver or unknown user enters your wireless network. Go to www.trendmicro.com.

A company called OTO makes Wi-Fi Defense 1.0, which is software to help you protect your wireless network. It automatically enables security settings for your WLAN and helps you monitor all the users currently on your network. It also makes it easy to add users to or remove users from your wireless network. Go to www.otosoftware.com.

Zone Labs has launched ZoneAlarm Wireless Security. The software automatically detects wireless networks and helps secure them. It also lets you set or configure different security settings for different wireless networks you commonly use. The software also includes a ZoneAlarm firewall. Go to www.zonelabs.com for more information.

LucidLink Wireless Security offers free software to help you set up a wireless home office. The product simplifies the steps necessary to set up and configure a wireless access point and to add and remove users of your WLAN. This software is free for up to three users; however, it requires that you also have a separate computer on a wired network to act as a security management console. This wired computer authorizes the wireless computers to connect to the wireless network. For more information, go to www.lucidlink.com.

9.3 Public Hotspot Safety

Wireless networks aren't just for the home. Many public places, including cafes, fast-food restaurants, hotels, town squares, bookstores, and libraries, offer wireless network connections. These public WLANs are called hotspots, and they reflect the incredible convenience of and demand for wireless connectivity. In fact, airplane manufacturer Boeing is now building aircraft equipped with wireless access points. These APs will pipe data to a satellite dish on the airplane, which will in turn beam that data to a collection of satellites and back down to a base station on Earth. The result? Passengers on properly equipped planes will be able to connect to the Internet at 35,000 feet using standard Wi-Fi-enabled laptops. (Currently this service is available from only a handful of airlines on select flights, but it may be coming to an aircraft near you soon.)

There are two ways to find public hotspots. The first is that a screen pops up on your laptop when your wireless network card or chip discovers a wireless network. Second, several services can help you find hotspots around the country. Intel offers both a national and international hotspot finder at http://intel. jiwire.com. If you like to surf the Internet while drinking coffee, you can search for Starbucks hotspots at www.starbucks.com/retail/wireless.asp. Another good option is www.wifinder.com, a global directory of 802.11b and 802.11g hotspots.

Some hotspots charge a fee for access, and you have to sign up for service. For instance, the T-Mobile HotSpot service charges $29.99 per month for unlimited wireless access at participating locations, which include Starbucks, Borders, and Kinkos. To help secure your connection, the T-Mobile service uses 802.1x, a security standard from the good people at the IEEE. Note that 802.1x is not an encryption standard. If you see that a wireless network is using 802.1x, this means only that it provides some measure of authentication. To encrypt the traffic, you also need to use WPA or SSL. (SSL stands for Secure Socket Layer. It's the protocol that enables encrypted transmission of information sent over the Web.) The T-Mobile service uses SSL.

Note that the Windows XP operating system has built-in support for 802.1x; it should be enabled by default. You can find out how to double-check if 802.1x is turned on in your computer by going to www.microsoft.com and typing **Set up 802.1x authentication** into the search field. The search will return several links to instructions for enabling 802.1x.

Unsecured Hotspots

The greatest danger Wi-Fi users face comes from hotspots that don't bother to turn on any of the encryption capabilities built into wireless APs. These unsecured hotspots are usually free to anyone who wants to join. The security capabilities aren't enabled to make it easier for users to get access. However, this also means that eavesdroppers can sniff your traffic and gather sensitive information.

If you're using a free public hotspot, you should take steps to secure the connection. Remember that your computer acts like a radio when you use a wireless network connection: All the data you generate is broadcast for anyone within range to intercept.

Several of these steps are general security best practices, such as ensuring that your firewall and anti-virus software are running (see Chapters 3, "Firewalls," and 4, "Getting Rid of Unwanted Guests, Part 1: Viruses and Worms," for more information). You should also turn off file sharing to prevent eavesdroppers from getting access to your documents over the Internet. Windows XP Service Pack 2 has file and printer sharing turned off by default. You can double-check this by clicking the Start button and then selecting Control Panel and Network and Internet Connections. Then click Network Setup Wizard (refer to Figure 9.1). You have to click through several questions until you get to the screen that asks about enabling file and printer sharing, as shown in Figure 9.4. If file and printer sharing is enabled, simply uncheck that box.

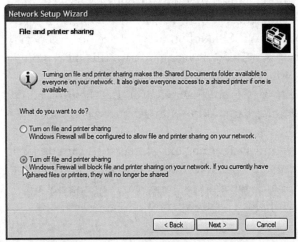

Figure 9.4   Turning off file and print sharing.

If the hotspot hasn't enabled WEP or WPA security settings, you can still protect your traffic with a Virtual Private Network (VPN). VPNs encrypt traffic between two points, such as firewalls at different branch locations of a corporation, or from a laptop back to a corporate network. VPNs were created to protect corporate traffic that travels across the public Internet from wired sniffers; they are in wide use today. By encrypting your wireless connection, you protect yourself from attackers with wireless sniffing tools.

If you're using a corporate-issued laptop with a preinstalled VPN client, you can use it to secure your wireless connection at an unsecured public hotspot. If you don't have a corporate-issued VPN client, you can sign up for HotSpotVPN (www.hotspotVPN.com), a service from a company called Wi-Fi Consulting. Pricing starts at $10.88 per month. You can also get one-, three-, and seven-day subscriptions starting at $3.88.

Evil Twins

Another potential hotspot danger is the evil twin attack. It works basically like this: an attacker places a laptop in the vicinity of a public hotspot. He or she then turns the laptop into a wireless AP and gives it the same network name (the same SSID) as the legitimate AP. If the imposter AP's signal is strong enough (or if the attacker disables the legitimate AP), the evil twin presents itself as a hotspot to other users. It may even present them with a logon screen that asks for a credit card number. If users then log onto this false AP, the attacker can steal any confidential information the user reveals while on the Internet.

There are several good defenses against evil twin attacks. The first is to configure your wireless software to not automatically connect to the nearest network. An even better solution is to activate the security features built into Wi-Fi technology (assuming that the hotspot has the security settings enabled). You can also make use of a VPN, as just described.

Note that a rash of evil twin attacks has yet to be reported, but it's important to be aware of the potential threats and to take the appropriate countermeasures ahead of time.

Don't Conduct Sensitive Transactions at a Hotspot

Your safest bet is to avoid conducting online banking and e-commerce while at a public hotspot. This should limit the potential damage if you are caught in an evil twin attack or another attempt to steal sensitive data over the airwaves.

9.4 Cell Phone and PDA Security

Cell phones, PDAs (Personal Digital Assistants), and wireless e-mail devices are convenient tools for communication and productivity, and they are rapidly converging on a variety of feature sets and capabilities. You can buy a PDA that includes a mobile phone and the ability to send and receive e-mail, and you can buy a cell phone with features such as Web browsing, e-mail access, calendaring, a digital camera, and text messaging (these souped-up cell phones are often called smart phones). Cell phones and PDAs can also use Wi-Fi or Bluetooth to connect to other mobile devices, regular PCs, and wireless networks.

As these tools burrow themselves deeper into the way we work and shop, they also become targets for miscreants and criminals. Pranksters may launch nuisance attacks that disrupt service or drain device batteries. However, cell phones and PDAs may also become targets of phishing attacks and other scams aimed at defrauding victims.

At present, mobile devices have remained relatively free of malware compared to their PC counterparts. However, mobile devices are beginning to coalesce around several common operating systems and communication vectors, which will make it easier for malware to spread. In fact, several cell phone and PDA viruses have emerged in the wild. So far these have mostly been "proof-of-concept" viruses with limited spread and no malicious payload.

We'll look at the basics of the mobile operating environment and the communication vectors that malware is likely to use to spread.

Mobile Operating Systems and Bluetooth

Mobile devices are converging on two operating systems: the PalmOS and Microsoft Windows Mobile (formerly Pocket PC). Cell phones are coalescing around the Symbian operating system (OS), which is a consortium of cell phone vendors. Symbian was developed in part to prevent Microsoft hegemony in the mobile phone world. As discussed in Chapter 4, malware has an easier time spreading if there's a small number of operating systems on a large number of devices. This is an inevitable outcome of standardization and interoperability requirements.

You should also know about Bluetooth. Bluetooth is a short-range (about 10 meters, or 32 feet) wireless technology that lets individual devices connect to form Personal Area Networks (PANs). Cell phones, PDAs, and laptops can use Bluetooth to connect to each other to transfer digital information, including files. Bluetooth is also used by mice, keyboards, and headsets. In addition, some automobiles are adding Bluetooth technology to allow for hands-free phone use.

Bluetooth technology is overseen by the Bluetooth Special Interest Group (SIG). The Bluetooth SIG was founded by well-known technology companies, including Nokia, Intel, and IBM. It currently boasts thousands of associate member companies. While Bluetooth offers great convenience for linking disparate products, it is also likely to become a popular infection vector for mobile malware.

Cell Phone Malware

Several kinds of malware have emerged that target so-called smart phones. We'll look at four examples and then discuss protection methods against these and other smart-phone malware:

- The Cabir worm appeared in June 2004. It targeted the Symbian mobile phone operating system and used Bluetooth to spread itself to other devices. The worm asked users to agree to accept a message. If the user accepted the message, he or she was prompted to install a file. Those who installed the file became infected with the worm. While the worm had no destructive payload, infected phones suffered reduced battery life as the worm continuously searched for other Bluetooth-enabled devices.

- The Skulls Trojan horse emerged in November 2004, and it also targeted the Symbian OS. To catch the Trojan horse, users had to download a program that was masquerading as a software utility to manage themes on the Nokia 7610 smart phone. If a user downloaded the program, named Extended Theme.SIS (SIS stands for Symbian Installation System), all the application icons were replaced with a skull-and-crossbones image. Users infected with this Trojan horse could still make outgoing calls and accept incoming calls, but all other applications were disabled. Some variants of this Trojan horse also added the Cabir worm to the payload.

- In January 2005, virus researchers discovered the Lasco A worm, which targeted the Symbian OS both via Bluetooth and if users shared infected SIS files. Users had to agree to install the file that contained the worm. The source code of the Lasco worm was very similar to that of the Cabir worm.

- The Mabir worm also targets the Symbian OS and can use Bluetooth to propagate. However, what sets this worm apart is that it can send infected files by MMS. MMS, which stands for Multimedia Message Service, is used to send digital media such as photos and audio files. Infected devices begin searching for other targets within range via Bluetooth.

Cell phones haven't suffered a major outbreak—the malware described here had very low infection rates. That said, it's clear that the know-how for writing cell phone viruses exists. All that remains to unleash a significant outbreak is for a malware writer to find the right combination of software and social engineering. Therefore, just as a wise person fixes a hole in the roof on a sunny day rather than waiting for the rain, smart phone users should take steps to protect themselves now before a clever or lucky virus writer releases a highly infectious program.

As shown in Table 9.2, several well-known anti-virus companies have released anti-virus software for mobile phones. (Symantec Mobile Security 4.0 also includes a firewall.) Anti-virus software protects you from known viruses. If your cell phone has a Web browser, you can download AV software directly to the phone. Otherwise, you can download the AV software to your computer and transfer it via a cable or Bluetooth connection. As of mid-2005, prices range from $15.95 to $44.95. Note that special offers or rebates may affect the final cost.

Securing Bluetooth

As you can infer from the malware described here, Bluetooth technology is a likely vector for smart-phone malware. Bluetooth-enabled devices allow you to choose higher or lower levels of security. This section describes various security

Table 9.2

Anti-Virus Software for PDAs and Mobile Phones

Product	Vendor	Platform	Operating Systems	Web Site
F-Secure Anti-Virus for Pocket PC	F-Secure	PDAs	Windows Mobile, Windows Pocket PC	www.f-secure.com
F-Secure Mobile Anti-Virus	F-Secure	Various Nokia mobile phones, N-Gage, SiemensSX1	Symbian OS	www.f-secure.com
Kaspersky AntiVirus Personal	Kaspersky Lab	PDAs	PalmOS, Windows Pocket PC	www.kaspersky.com
PC-cillin for Wireless	Trend Micro	PDAs	PalmOS, Windows Pocket PC	www.trendmicro.com
Symantec AntiVirus for Handhelds	Symantec	PDAs	PalmOS, Windows Mobile, Pocket PC	www.symantec.com
Symantec Mobile Security 4.0	Symantec	Smart phones	Symbian OS	www.symantec.com
Trend Micro Mobile Security	Trend Micro	Smart phones	Windows Mobile for Pocket PC Phone edition, Windows Mobile for Smartphones, Symbian OS	www.trendmicro.com

settings, but you have to refer to your owner's manual to find out how to make the adjustments.

If you don't use Bluetooth, the simplest and most secure option is to disable it.

If you do use Bluetooth, you can set your smart phone visibility to Hidden or nondiscoverable mode. This prevents any infected devices within range from sending malware to you. Refer to your Bluetooth-enabled device's manual to find out how to set it to Hidden.

Bluetooth also allows you to create security pairings between Bluetooth devices, such as a mobile phone and a headset. A persistent security pairing encrypts any communication between the two devices. However, you should be wary of pairing with untrusted devices. If you do set up a pairing, use the Unauthorized setting; this ensures that you get to authorize any connection request.

Finally, if you do have Bluetooth enabled, be wary of accepting unsolicited files or applications. If you receive a file when you weren't expecting one, the safest option is to reject or delete it.

PDA Security

PDAs are becoming increasingly popular targets for thieves because they often store sensitive information, such as names and phone numbers, PINs, account numbers, and even Social Security numbers. PDAs that use Bluetooth face many of the same vulnerabilities that smart phones do, including the spread of malware. As shown in Table 9.2, several companies offer anti-virus software for handheld devices because some of the viruses that target smart phones can also infect PDAs.

Until now, very little malware has targeted PDAs. In August 2004, researchers discovered the Brador Trojan horse, which targeted the Windows Mobile 2003/ Pocket PC operating system. While security researchers had created "proof-of-concept" PDA malware in the lab, Brador was the first example of PDA malware found in the wild. When successfully installed, this Trojan horse allowed a remote attacker to upload and download files to and from the PDA. While Brador had a very low infection rate, it demonstrated that malware writers had the ability and inclination to target Microsoft-based handhelds.

However, the greatest danger that PDA users face is physical, not technological. Even though PDAs are easily lost or stolen, many users don't bother to password-protect access to sensitive information. Thus, a thief who gets his or her hands on your PDA will have access to whatever personal data you've stored on the device. Be sure to use the password function to protect your information. Choose a password that combines letters and numbers; this makes it more difficult for the thief to crack the password. You should also refrain from storing sensitive information such as account numbers or your Social Security number on the device. If you do need to keep such information on the device, consider using a software encryption program available for PDAs that can be used as an extra layer of security to protect the data.

9.5 VoIP Security

Voice over Internet Protocol (VoIP) is a new technology for making telephone calls over the Internet. Traditional telephone calls set up a dedicated circuit between two telephones, and the speakers' voices are transmitted as digital signals across this circuit. By contrast, VoIP doesn't require a dedicated circuit between two callers. Instead, it takes the speakers' voices and breaks them into individual packets that get routed across the public Internet in the same way as e-mail and Web traffic. (For more on how IP works, see Chapter 3.)

Several companies, including Vonage, Packet8, Verizon, and SBC, offer consumer VoIP solutions that cost less than standard phone service. These VoIP services require you to buy a special adapter, into which you plug your telephone and your broadband (that is, cable or DSL) Internet connection.

Another option is Skype software (www.skype.com), which enables you to make free phone calls from your computer to other Skype users. Skype works on Windows, Macintosh, and Linux. All you need is a headset with a microphone that you can plug into your computer and an Internet connection. There have been more than 108 million Skype downloads so far. Skype also offers a paid service called SkypeOut that lets you make calls from your computer to regular telephones.

Although VoIP represents a less expensive way to make telephone calls, it presents several potential security issues. First, it requires you to open a broad range of outbound ports and a smaller range of inbound ports on your firewall. Attackers or automated malware may attempt to exploit these open ports to gain access to your computer. At this point there have been no reports of widespread attempts to exploit VoIP's open ports, but as more consumers sign on for such services, these attempts are highly likely. Also, because VoIP relies on your Internet connection, any attacks against that connection may cut off your VoIP phone service. In addition, if your Internet service provider suffers an outage of any kind (for instance, a power outage, or perhaps a service outage caused by a denial-of-service attack), your VoIP phone service will be affected.

VoIP and 911

A more significant issue for VoIP has to do with 911 emergency calls. When you dial 911 using the traditional phone system, it automatically associates your phone number with your name and address and provides this information to the emergency dispatcher at the appropriate Public Service Answering Point (PSAP). PSAPs are the first point of contact for emergency calls. They are often located at police or fire stations, although in some cases a PSAP may forward an emergency call to the appropriate public safety agency. Because the traditional phone service can display a name and address to the dispatcher, emergency responders can still be sent to the scene even if the caller is incapacitated or otherwise unable to provide the information.

However, because VoIP technology bypasses the traditional telephone network, your name and address aren't automatically linked to your phone number and are not automatically provided to the emergency dispatcher. In fact, some VoIP consumer services don't automatically have 911 dialing enabled. You have to enable this feature manually, and in some cases you have to pay extra for the service. Consult your user documentation to find out how to enable 911 dialing on your VoIP service.

In addition, you have to register your location with your VoIP provider so that the provider can route your call to the appropriate PSAP. If you provide an incorrect address, or if you use your VoIP service at a different location than the one you've listed with your provider, your VoIP 911 call will not be routed to the correct PSAP.

Also note that you may still have to tell the emergency dispatcher your name, phone number, and address if you are using VoIP 911 dialing. That's because some VoIP 911 dialing systems route your call to a general PSAP number, not the emergency response center.

Finally, as mentioned, your VoIP service will not function during power outages, so even if you've enabled 911 dialing, you won't be able to make or receive any VoIP calls.

The Federal Communications Commission is developing plans to require all VoIP providers to provide 911 calling capability. In addition, VoIP providers are working to establish automatic 911 calling capabilities. At present, however, if you use VoIP you may have to manually enable emergency 911 dialing.

9.6 Checklist

Use this checklist as a quick-reference guide to the material covered in this chapter.

Do

- Remember that a wireless network broadcasts radio signals that can be picked up by other wireless computing equipment.
- Turn on WEP or WPA to encrypt your wireless traffic, and ensure that only authorized users connect to your access point.
- Take additional steps to protect your wireless network, including changing the SSID.
- Use a firewall, and turn off file sharing when using a public hotspot.
- Consider using anti-virus software on your smart phone and PDA.
- Use a password to protect the information on your PDA if it gets stolen.
- Activate 911 dialing if you use VoIP.

Don't

- Use the default SSID or passwords when setting up a wireless network.
- Conduct sensitive transactions such as online banking or e-commerce purchases at public hotspots.
- Forget to activate 911 dialing if you use VoIP.

9.7 Helpful Resources

This section presents additional resources to help you learn more.

If you're looking for more information about Wi-Fi technology and products, a great place to start is Wi-Fi Planet at www.wi-fiplanet.com. The site includes tutorials, product reviews, security information, and more.

You can find a helpful chart that provides more information about the 802.11b, g, and a wireless standards at www.linksys.com/edu/wirelessstandards.asp.

Microsoft has information about wireless networking and security, including tips on staying safe at public hotspots. Go to www.microsoft.com/atwork/ stayconnected/hotspots.mspx to find out more.

Intel offers wireless security tips at www.intel.com/personal/do_more/ wireless/security/.

Chapter 10

Privacy and the Internet

We live in an age of relentless data collection and analysis. The electronic networks that underpin so much of our commerce and communications also enable unprecedented harvesting, storing, and sharing (or selling) of personal information. Two forces drive this harvesting engine, one commercial and the other governmental. Each force has its own motives and each its own resources (although in many cases those resources are converging), but they both draw from a common source: you and me.

In the commercial arena, data brokers stockpile databases with significant facts such as your Social Security number, birth date, marital status, and monthly mortgage payments, as well as seemingly worthless information such as your preference in toothpaste. These data points are gathered and traded or sold to various parties. In turn, these parties analyze the data in hopes of gleaning essential, actionable information. Is this person a credit risk? Does this job applicant have a criminal record? Might this consumer be interested in receiving information about a new brand of toothpaste?

On the government side there's a long tradition of intelligence gathering on the domestic and international fronts by law enforcement and espionage agencies. This intelligence is used to gain advantages in diplomacy, commerce, crime fighting, war, and national security. Fifty years ago significant government resources were poured into an information-gathering infrastructure to fight the Cold War.

These days the major impetus for widespread data gathering is the fight against terrorism.

For the most part, we citizens benefit from the commercial and governmental impulse to harvest information. Data brokers make it easier to get loans, buy a house or rent an apartment, get notified of strange activity on our credit cards, and so on. They also enable us to take advantage of commercial competition (such as getting a coupon for a different brand of toothpaste) and corporate cooperation (such as getting airline miles for credit card purchases). Meanwhile, local, state, and federal agencies can track and share information to catch criminals and fight fraud. The government also hopes that information gathered by law enforcement and anti-terrorism agencies may prevent a repeat of the 9/11 attacks.

But this massive data gathering has a shadowy side, one that conjures conspiracy theories of sinister corporate cabals dictating global affairs, or Orwellian scenarios of omniscient, omnipresent state surveillance. The problem is that these scenarios contain a germ of truth. Chapter 2, "Preventing Identity Theft," briefly mentioned the ChoicePoint scandal, in which the data broker ChoicePoint announced that it had sold sensitive personal information from about 145,000 people to identity thieves posing as legitimate business owners. This scandal revealed to Americans just how much information is being gathered about them— and how much money is made selling that information. Privacy advocates point to government-sponsored data-gathering systems such as Echelon (a global electronic surveillance system run in part by the National Security Agency [NSA]) and Carnivore (a program that lets U.S. law enforcement agencies sift through e-mail and other Internet communications). The fact is that the benefits of the data engine come at a price: the erosion of privacy regarding our habits, preferences, and personal information, and the very real possibility that such information will be misused.

For instance, identity thieves routinely manipulate the guardians of data to open fraudulent accounts. Innocent citizens are barred from boarding airplanes because their names trigger matches on "no-fly" terrorist watch lists. (Even the powerful aren't immune from such mistakes. In 2004, Senator Ted Kennedy, perhaps one of the most recognizable politicians in the U.S., was held up at an airport for precisely this reason.)

Mistaken information can also have political repercussions. In the 2000 presidential elections, hundreds of voters were turned away from Florida polling stations because they were mistakenly listed as ex-felons who had lost the right to vote. And in the war on terror, innocent persons have been detained without legal representation.

Unfortunately, the genie is out of the bottle with regard to data gathering. However, you can take steps to gain some amount of privacy, at least online. This chapter examines different ways of reclaiming, or asserting, your privacy rights on the Internet. We'll also show you how to uncover what information is being collected about you by major data brokers.

10.1 Internet Privacy Options

It's possible to attain a fair measure of privacy when it comes to your Internet usage. Software exists that can encrypt the e-mail and instant messages you send and the files and folders you save on your computer. In addition, Web anonymizers can help obfuscate the sites you visit.

Encryption is a process by which information (otherwise known as plaintext) gets run through a mathematical algorithm to produce gibberish (ciphertext). The only way to transform the ciphertext back to plaintext is through the use of a key. The key is like a secret code that is combined with another mathematical operation to reassemble the ciphertext into plaintext. As discussed in several other chapters, the Internet relies on encryption for e-commerce and to authenticate parties that might not have a mechanism for establishing trust or exchanging identification credentials in the real world.

Cryptography Basics

Generally speaking, there are two kinds of digital encryption: symmetric and asymmetric. In symmetric cryptography the same key is used to encrypt plaintext and decrypt ciphertext. The security of the cryptography is dependent in part on the algorithm used and the key's length. The U.S. standard algorithm is called Advanced Encryption Standard (AES). This algorithm supports keys of various lengths. Key length is measured in bits. The strength of the key length is judged by how long it would take a commercially available computer to decipher an encrypted message by trying every possible combination of letters and numbers. This is known as a brute-force attack, and it's the least-elegant method of breaking a cipher. However, it makes a good measurement, because you have to assume that your adversary has access to widely available computing technology.

In this day and age, 40-bit keys are regarded as useless; 128-bit, 256-bit, and 512-bit keys are industrial-grade; 1024-bit keys are paranoid-grade; and 2048-bit keys are for people who could tell you what they've encrypted but then would have to kill you.

Symmetric cryptography is well-suited for encrypting data, such as files, folders, and documents. The problem with symmetric cryptography is that it's less useful for sending encrypted messages. You can't include the key with the message because anyone who intercepts the message can simply use the key to decrypt it. (Cryptologists *always* assume that someone is snooping on them.)You could put the key on a disk and mail it, but then you risk the disk's being lost or intercepted. You could arrange a drop-off place for the disk, but if your adversary is monitoring your communications, he or she will know where and when to snatch it. And even if you can arrange a drop-off in secret, what if your correspondent lives on the other side of the country? You could bring the disk to your correspondent, but in that case you could just deliver the message itself and not bother with all the encryption.

The solution to this problem is asymmetric cryptography, which is also called public key cryptography. In public key cryptography, a single mathematical function generates two keys: One key is used to encrypt plaintext, and a separate key is used to decrypt it. The key that encrypts the plaintext can't be used to decrypt it, and vice versa. The fact that such an operation is possible is quite stunning in itself. A lot of complicated mathematics are behind public key cryptography (as evidenced by the fact that the three people who discovered the most popular public key algorithm, known as RSA, were all at MIT). For our purposes, all you need to understand is that the two keys solve the problem of how to securely exchange a symmetric key.

The basic idea works like this: Alice generates a public key pair. She keeps one of these keys private, and she publishes the other key in a public directory on the Internet. If Bob wants to send Alice an encrypted message, he simply looks up her public key in the directory and uses it to encrypt the message. When Alice receives the message, she uses her private key to decrypt it. If Alice wants to reply to Bob, she looks up Bob's public key and uses that to encrypt the message.

As an added layer of security, rather than simply using Alice's public key to encrypt the message, Bob can use a strong symmetric key to encrypt the message and then use Alice's public key to encrypt the symmetric key. Then he sends both chunks of ciphertext to Alice. Alice uses her private key to decrypt the symmetric key and then uses the symmetric key to decrypt the message.

Digital Signatures and Digital Certificates

Confused yet? If not, here's where things get tricky. Public key cryptography also enables the use of digital signatures and digital certificates. A digital signature serves two purposes. First, it verifies that a message has come from the person who claims to have sent it. Second, it prevents the message from being tampered with.

To create a digital signature, Alice takes her unencrypted message and runs it through a hash algorithm. A hash algorithm is a mathematical process that generates a message digest. What's neat about the hash algorithm is that if you run the same message through the same hash algorithm a thousand times, you get exactly the same message digest each time. However, if you change even one letter in the message and then run it through the hash algorithm, you get a different message digest. Thus, if you send the message and a message digest (and the hashing algorithm you used) to your correspondent, he or she can then run the same hashing algorithm on the message. If the two message digests match, the correspondent can be assured that the message hasn't been changed.

So Alice runs her message through the hash algorithm and gets a message digest. She takes this message digest and encrypts it with her own *private* key. Bob can then use Alice's public key to decrypt the ciphertext. A successful decryption indicates to Bob that the message did in fact come from Alice, because only Alice has access to her private key. Digital signatures are not meant to protect a message from eavesdroppers; digital signatures authenticate the sender and prove the message's integrity.

Of course, one problem with public key technology is how to prove that the owner of the public key is who she says she is. For instance, there's nothing stopping Eve from publishing her own public key but labeling it as Alice's public key. Thus, Bob thinks he's sending a protected message to Alice, but in fact he's sending it to Eve. (And you thought Fox Mulder was paranoid? He's got nothing on cryptologists.)

This is where digital certificates come in. A digital certificate contains a person or organization's public key. Digital certificates are issued by a trusted third party (called a Certificate Authority), and they act as a form of electronic authentication to verify that the holder of the certificate is who it claims to be. One way to think of a digital certificate is like a driver's license. It's issued by a trusted entity and offers reasonably strong proof that you are who you say you are.

Of course, even drivers' licenses can be faked, so if you're wondering how you can trust the organization that issued the digital certificate, you're finally learning to think like a cryptologist. Fraudulent digital certificates have been issued in the past, and it's likely this will happen again. However, the trust chain needs to end (or begin) somewhere, and several companies, including one called VeriSign, do a good business acting as Certificate Authorities and issuing digital certificates for the Internet community.

While all of this rigmarole sounds so complicated as to be impractical for the real world, public key encryption actually works. The Internet's entire e-commerce structure is based on public key technology; every time you buy something from Amazon.com or conduct an online banking transaction, you are using the public key infrastructure.

Public key encryption also plays an important role in a popular form of e-mail encryption, which we'll discuss next.

E-Mail Encryption

The most popular implementation of public key technology for e-mail encryption is called PGP. PGP stands for Pretty Good Privacy and was created by Phil Zimmermann. It's also the name of the corporation that makes commercial encryption software, including PGP Desktop Home 9.0. This product can be used to encrypt outgoing e-mails, AOL Instant Messenger messages, and some files on your PC. It supports Microsoft Outlook and Thunderbird, the e-mail client developed by the Mozilla Foundation, which also makes the Firefox Web browser. It's available online at www.pgpstore.com.

You can also download a free, open-source version of the software called Open PGP at www.pgpi.org. You have to click through several pages to find the Windows XP version.

You can also get an e-mail encryption solution from a company called Hushmail. Hushmail uses the Open PGP standard and offers both a Web mail version and a version that works with Outlook, the e-mail client that is built into Microsoft Office. Find out more at www.hushmail.com.

In addition to third-party software, the Outlook e-mail client that comes with Microsoft Office allows you to encrypt outgoing e-mail messages. It's also based on public key technology, so you have to download and purchase a digital certificate. The first time you try to send an encrypted message, Microsoft walks you through the steps necessary to obtain that digital certificate.

However, before you go through all these steps, be aware that you may not be able to send encrypted messages using Outlook unless your correspondents have also created digital signatures and registered them in a public online directory. That's because, if you remember from our discussion of public key cryptography, the sender needs to use the recipient's public key for the transaction to work. If you can convince your correspondents to buy their own digital certificates, here are the steps you need to take to use e-mail encryption in Outlook.

First, open Outlook and compose your message. Once your message is ready, click the Options button, as shown in Figure 10.1. When the Message Options window opens, as shown in Figure 10.2, click the Security Settings button. The Security Properties window opens, as shown in Figure 10.3. Check the Encrypt message contents and attachments checkbox. For the time being you should not check the Add digital signature to this message checkbox, because you first need to install a digital certificate. Click OK in the Security Properties dialog box. You should be returned to your message. Choose an address to send the message to.

Figure 10.1   Clicking the Options button after composing a message in Outlook.

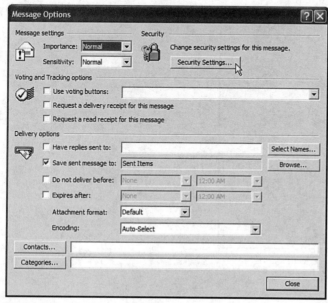

Figure 10.2   The Message Options dialog box.

Figure 10.3   The Security Properties dialog box.

After you've typed your message, click the Send button. You see the Welcome to Secure E-mail window as shown in Figure 10.4. Click the Get Digital ID... button. This takes you to a Microsoft Web site with links to two digital certificate providers: GeoTrust and VeriSign.

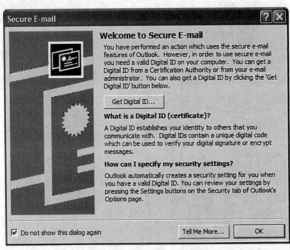

Figure 10.4   The Welcome to Secure E-Mail dialog box.

GeoTrust's Personal Digital ID lets you digitally sign Word documents and digitally sign and encrypt e-mail. It costs $19.95 per year.

VeriSign's Digital ID is also $19.95 per year. You get $1,000 worth of protection against economic loss if your digital certificate gets corrupted, lost, or misused. VeriSign also lists you in a public directory so that anyone who wants to send you an encrypted message can find your public key. It also allows for free lookup of any other VeriSign-issued digital certificate. VeriSign also offers a free 60-day trial of the digital certificate.

You have to register for the certificate. You need access to your e-mail (and your telephone for GeoTrust) for the registration process. The registration is fairly simple; it asks you to provide your name and e-mail address. After the registration, you click an installation button to install the digital certificate. When you start the installation, Microsoft may display a Potential Scripting Violation warning. Click Yes to continue.

Once you get the digital certificate installed, you can finally click the Send button in Microsoft Outlook. However, as mentioned, you may run into snags if the people you are sending encrypted messages to don't have digital certificates (see Figure 10.5). In addition, some mail systems don't support or have disabled S/MIME (Secure/Multipurpose Internet Mail Extensions, a public key encryption standard), or they may not accept encrypted messages because anti-virus scanners can't scan encrypted e-mail.

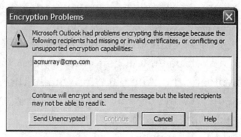

Figure 10.5   The Encryption Problems dialog box.

File and Folder Encryption

Desktop encryption is a good idea if you keep sensitive information, such as online tax returns, account numbers, and so on, on your computer. In particular, encrypting this information provides you with some protection if your computer is lost or stolen. (According to a 2001 survey, thousands of laptops are forgotten in London cabs.)

Most desktop encryption products work along the same lines. You designate a file or folder to be encrypted. To decrypt it, you are prompted to provide a password. This is how Icon Lock-iT XP works. Go to www.iconlockit.com for more information. As mentioned, PGP Desktop includes e-mail and file encryption. You can also find encryption utilities online. For instance, *PC Magazine* has an encryption utility called File Warden 2. For a free download, simply go to www.pcmagazine.com and search for File Warden 2.

Web Anonymizers

Web anonymizers can help protect your privacy while you use the Internet. Anonymizing products remove information that could be used to identify you and track your Web surfing habits. They also route your Web traffic through a variety of routers and servers to obfuscate the source and destination (this is sometimes called onion routing). The Center for Democracy and Technology provides a long list of Web anonymizing services at www.cdt.org/resourcelibrary/Privacy/Tools/Anonymizer/.

You can also check out an anonymizing program called Tor. Tor is sponsored by the Electronic Frontier Foundation (EFF), a privacy rights advocacy group. To learn more, go to http://tor.eff.org/.

Another option is Privoxy, at www.privoxy.org. Privoxy is a Web proxy that can strip out ads, banners, and pop-ups and manage cookies. A proxy is a machine that mediates Internet connections for other computers. That is, instead of going directly to a Web server to download a Web page, you go to the proxy instead. The proxy goes to the server and downloads the Web page for you. In the meantime, the proxy can remove any unwanted elements at your request. It also interferes with tracking cookies. The Web server can't place a cookie on your computer because your computer never visited the Web page.

Another way to regain some Internet privacy is to remove tracking cookies from your computer. Tracking cookies record the Web sites you visit and the ads you click inside a text file stored on your computer. Tracking cookies are used to gather information about your surfing habits for the purpose of delivering targeted advertising and gathering statistics about Web pages you visit. All Web sites you visit set cookies on your computer to help the Web server remember where you are on a site and to personalize Web site environments by "remembering" your preferences and settings. However, tracking cookies share that information with third parties. These cookies won't harm your computer, but they do represent an intrusion into your privacy. You can detect, remove, and block tracking cookies using anti-spyware software (see Chapter 5, "Getting Rid of Unwanted Guests, Part 2: Spyware, Adware, and Trojan Horses").

10.2 Dealing with Data Brokers

Data brokers such as ChoicePoint, LexisNexis, and Acxiom gather incredible amounts of information about us. These companies perform their own data collection from public sources, such as telephone directories and records of public home sales, which are public information. But they also get data from third-party sources. For instance, Acxiom gets much of its information from companies that want to mine that information to learn more about their customers. According to author Robert Harrow, Jr., in his book *No Place to Hide*, companies including Sears, Hallmark Cards, Safeway, and Lands End all send the information they've accumulated on their customers to Acxiom. On top of that, banks and credit card companies also pipe their data into Acxiom's databases.

The problem for consumers is that while you may take steps to limit the information you provide to individual businesses and government agencies, those same entities can load all those disparate pieces of information about you into a massive computer system that can correlate and analyze huge amounts of information.

One way to avoid having a dossier, or at least a detailed dossier, built up is to keep as much information about yourself as possible out of the public record. Chris Hoofnagle, West Coast director of the Electronic Privacy Information Center (EPIC), a privacy advocacy organization, offers these tips:

- If you buy or sell a home, make sure your Social Security number and date of birth don't appear in the public record.

- When you sign up for telephone service and public utilities, insist that the company not use your Social Security number or driver's license number. You may have to pay a deposit if you take this route.

- Don't get arrested because arrest records can be made public.

You can also take steps to restrict what the data brokers do with that information, and in some cases you can get access to the information they hold about you, opt out of databases, or have information removed.

Acxiom (www.acxiom.com)

Acxiom has two basic product sets: InfoBase Marketing, and InfoBase and Sentricx Reference. Acxiom's clients use InfoBase Marketing to create lists for targeted advertising. InfoBase Marketing does not include credit or medical information or Social Security numbers. You can opt out of the InfoBase Marketing database, which means that businesses that you patronize cannot access your information through Acxiom, and you will not receive telemarketing calls, direct mail (aka junk mail), catalogs, or e-mail from companies that do business with Acxiom. You can request an opt-out form by calling 501-342-2722 or 877-774-2094 or by sending an e-mail to optoutUS@acxiom.com.

Acxiom's InfoBase and Sentricx Reference services do include financial information and Social Security numbers. Acxiom clients use these services for things like employee screening and issuing mortgages. Law enforcement agencies can also get access to InfoBase and Sentricx Reference information. You can access information being stored about you by requesting a Reference Information Report. Note that Acxiom charges a $5 fee. You can request a report by calling 501-342-2722 or 877-774-2094 or by sending an e-mail to referencereport@acxiom.com.

To get more information, go to www.acxiom.com and click the Privacy link on the left side of the home page. You can also type **Notice, Access, Choice** (just as I've written it here) into the search field on the home page to get more information about access to the information Acxiom collects about you.

ChoicePoint (www.choicepoint.com)

The Fair and Accurate Credit Transactions (FACT) Act entitles consumers to an annual free report from consumer reporting agencies. According to ChoicePoint, three of its services fall under the FACT Act: C.L.U.E., which tracks information on insurance claims histories; ChoicePoint WorkPlace Solutions, which covers employment history; and Resident Data, which maintains tenant history information. Under the provision of the FACT Act, ChoicePoint is required to provide, upon request, one free copy per year of your consumer profile from each of these business units. Note that these business units may not have a consumer file on you. However, if you'd like to check, you have the following options (you can also get more information at www.choicepoint.com/factact.html):

- To request copies of your claims history report, visit www.choicetrust.com or call 866-312-8076.

- To request a copy of your employment history report, call 866-312-8075.

- To request a copy of your tenant history report, call 877-448-5732.

You can also request this information by regular mail. You have to send your name and address to the respective business units listed here. They will send you a request form that you have to fill out and return.

For claims history reports:

ChoicePoint Consumer Disclosure Center

P.O. Box 105295

Atlanta, GA 30348

For employment history reports:

ChoicePoint WorkPlace Solutions Consumer Disclosure Center

P.O. Box 105292

Atlanta, GA 30348

For tenant history reports:

Resident Data Consumer Disclosure Center

P.O. Box 850126

Richardson, TX 75085-0126

LexisNexis (www.lexisnexis.com)

LexisNexis provides legal and business information and stores news, public records, and more. You can discover what nonpublic information is being stored about you by requesting a copy of your information. LexisNexis charges $8 for the service. To request a copy of your information, write to

LexisNexis Consumer Access Program

P.O. Box 933

Dayton, OH 45401

You have to include the $8 in the request. You also have to list your name, maiden name, nicknames, and any aliases you've had. You can also include your Social Security number, which LexisNexis says will help fulfill your information request. However, the Social Security number is optional. For more information about getting your personal information, go to www.lexisnexis.com/terms/privacy/data/obtain.asp.

You can request that LexisNexis voluntarily remove nonpublic records about you. However, the company insists that one of three conditions be met: You must be a law enforcement officer who might be endangered by having your information in a database, you must be a victim of identity theft and have a copy of the police report and an Identity Theft Affidavit (see Chapter 2 for more information), or you must be at risk of physical harm and have a protective court order or police report to prove it. To find out more about meeting these conditions and requesting record removal, go to www.lexisnexis.com/terms/privacy/data/remove.asp.

10.3 Checklist

Use this checklist as a quick-reference guide to the material covered in this chapter.

Do

- Consider using e-mail encryption to protect your messages from eavesdroppers.
- Consider using Web anonymizers or proxies to hide your Web surfing activities.
- Try to keep your Social Security number and birth date out of public records.
- Check for dossiers that might be kept about you at major data brokers.
- Opt out from data brokers' information-sharing programs wherever possible.

Don't

- Include sensitive information on public records wherever possible.
- Forget that you and your correspondents need to sign up for digital certificates to use public key encryption systems.

10.4 Helpful Resources

This section presents additional resources to help you learn more.

The Electronic Privacy Information Center (EPIC) is a public research interest group that studies civil liberties and privacy issues. The center publishes reports and books on privacy, open government, and free speech. EPIC members often testify before state and federal legislative committees regarding privacy and civil liberties legislation. The EPIC Web site has loads of news stories and information about privacy issues. Two pages of particular interest are the list of Internet privacy tools. Go to www.epic.org/privacy/tools.html. Note that EPIC does not endorse any of the tools listed. It is simply a sample of available tools. You should also check out Top Ten Consumer Privacy Resolutions. Go to www.epic.org/privacy/2004tips.html.

The Center for Democracy & Technology is a nonprofit advocacy group that works to protect citizens' liberties, particularly free expression and privacy. CDT members regularly testify before Congress on important issues like privacy, free expression, and copyright. The Web site is a great resource for staying abreast of legislation. You'll find books, articles, and news items, as well as links for contacting members of the Senate and House regarding various issues. Go to www.cdt.org.

The Electronic Frontier Foundation (EFF) is another nonprofit that advocates for protecting our liberties in a highly technological world. The EFF tracks issues such as privacy, copyright, file sharing, e-voting, and so on. You can find out more at www.eff.org.

The Privacy Rights Clearinghouse is a resource for information about Internet privacy, financial privacy, and other subjects. It offers tips for protecting your privacy and tracks privacy-related federal legislation. Go to www.privacyrights.org.

The Code Book: The Science of Secrecy from Ancient Egypt to Quantum Cryptography, by Simon Singh, is an excellent and highly readable introduction to cryptography. Singh tracks the origins of cryptography and cryptanalysis through to the near-present day. Along the way he demonstrates the historical role that ciphering played in the death of Mary Queen of Scotts, the Allied victory in World War II, the development of modern computing, the creation of public key cryptography and PGP, and the current struggle between governments wary of publicly available cryptographic technology and researchers leery of government surveillance.

No Place to Hide: Behind the Scenes of Our Emerging Surveillance Society, by Robert O'Harrow, Jr., illuminates the extent of commercial and governmental data harvesting and explores how the private and government sectors are collaborating to create a national intelligence infrastructure.

Chatter: Dispatches from the Secret World of Global Eavesdropping, by Patrick Radden Keefe, explores the depths of global governmental surveillance and the conundrum of security and privacy. It's also a first-rate introduction to Echelon, the NSA-operated global electronic surveillance system developed by the U.S., Britain, Canada, Australia, and New Zealand.

Conclusion

Thanks for reading this book. We hope we've helped you understand Internet security risks and provided some practical information about how to protect yourself and your family while online.

Surfing the Web can be as safe as walking around your neighborhood. With the right tools and training, you can avoid many of the pitfalls and dangers that lead to financial losses, lost data, and reduced PC performance, or just plain annoyance.

Today, spyware, spam, and Internet fraud capture the headlines. But technology is always changing, and the future is likely to bring new risks and threats along with the latest software and cool new capabilities. The good news is that many of the best practices and advice in this book will apply to new threats as well as to the risks we've covered in the previous chapters.

As a final reminder, we've listed five basic steps you can take that will make your PC safe against today's and tomorrow's attacks:

1. Use an Internet security solution that combines anti-virus, anti-spyware, firewall, intrusion detection, and vulnerability management for maximum protection against blended threats. Keep your security subscription service up to date so that you can receive the most current virus/spyware definitions.

2. Update your operating system and web browser software regularly. Remember that the second Tuesday of every month is Patch Tuesday, when Microsoft rolls out the latest software fixes. Make it a habit to get these updates installed right away, or turn on the Automatic Updates function in Windows XP. Also remember to use passwords that combine letters and numbers.

3. Don't take candy from strangers. By this we mean you should be suspicious, or at least cautious, when using the Internet. Be especially wary of "free" programs that promise to do something amusing or helpful. Be very suspicious of e-mail. Don't open messages from people you don't know. If you do open messages from people you don't know, don't activate or download or click anything they've attached to the e-mail. Do not e-mail sensitive information such as passwords, credit card and bank account numbers, or your Social Security number to anyone, ever.

4. Don't buy anything from a spammer. Be aware of the dangers associated with purchasing software—or any product—via suspicious e-mail. The software could come with viruses or bugs that can be destructive to your computer's operating system. Don't sign up on unknown Web sites that promise to remove your name from spam lists, and don't click the "remove from mailing list" link in an e-mail; these are tricks spammers use to verify and obtain e-mail addresses.

5. Perform regular backups of your essential files to prevent losing data in the event of a serious computer problem. You can save files to CDs, flash drives, or with an online storage service.

If five rules are too many, we can distill them to one: Use your common sense. The Internet is not your friend. It is a community, and just like any community, a percentage of its population is made up of thieves, con artists, criminals, and vandals. By no means should you avoid the Internet; rather, treat it as you would a strange part of town—keep your eyes open, use your head, and keep one hand on your wallet.

Index

Sygate Personal Firewall Pro, 42
Sygate Personal Firewall Standard, 43
Symantec
   AntiVirus for Handhelds, 188
   Mobile Security 4.0, 188
   Norton AntiVirus, 60
   Security Check, 44, 59, 143
   Spyware Edition, 84
   unwanted software study, 73
symmetric cryptography, 197-198

T

Takedown: The Pursuit and Capture of Kevin Mitnick, 12
TCP (Transmission Control Protocol), 29-30
telephone fraud, 21
Tenebril, SpyCatcher, 83
testing firewalls, 44-45
thefts, identity, 9-10
   author personal experience, 24-25
   dos and don'ts, 20-21
   methods, 10-14
   prevention, 14-19
   recovery, 19-20
   resources, 21-22
Thomas Web site, 77
threats, 2
   Adware, 4-5
   identity theft, 3
   reasons for, 5-7
   spam, 3
   Spyware, 4-5
   Trojan Horses, 4-5
   viruses, 4
   worms, 4
Titanium Antivirus, 61
tokens, security, 17-18
tools, identity theft prevention, 15-16
tracking cookies, 78
Transmission Control Protocol (TCP), 29-30
TransUnion, 15
Trend Micro, 60
   House Call, 59
   Mobile Security, 188
   Wi-Fi Intrusion Detection, 182
tricklers, 74
Trojan Horses, 4-5
   defining, 67-72
   dos and don'ts, 95-96
   how infects computer, 80-82
   protecting against, 82-92

removing, 92-95
resources, 96
Trusted Sites, 134
two-factor authentication, 17-18

U-V

updates
   automatic, Windows XP Service Pack 2, 39, 130-131
   software, 91-92

VeriSign, Digital ID, 203
Virtual Private Network (VPNs), 184
Virus Bulletin Web site, 62
Virus List Web site, 62
viruses, 4, 50-52
   anti-virus software, 54-56
   Beagle.BA, 63-66
   capabilities, 53
   dos and don'ts, 62
   infection recovery, 59-60
   protecting against, 56-58
   resources, 62-63
   selecting anti-virus software, 60, 62
   Windows XP Service Pack 2, 39, 127-128
VirusScan, 60-61
Visa Web site, 21
Vista operating system, 143
Voice over IP. *See* VoIP
VoIP (Voice over IP), 29, 173
   dos and don'ts, 192
   resources, 192
   security, 190-191
   wireless networks, 174-182
VPNs (Virtual Private Networks), 184

W

Web, 147-148
   anonymizers, 204-205
   beacons, 106
   browsers. *See* browsers
   bugs, 106
   dos and don'ts, 170
   file sharing, 164-169
   filtering content, 148-160
   resources, 170-171
   security steps, 211-212
   sexual predators, 160-165
Web sites
   Acxiom, 206
   Anti-Phishing Working Group (APWG), 22